K

Praise for the book

This book is unique since it covers different areas such as innovation processes, service quality control, human resource management and strategy in action which together contribute to exceptional performance. To learn from excellent business results you need to understand the game behind the success, the roles of the game, the strategies and tactics chosen. The authors' findings from studying Singapore Airlines are presented in an inspiring and pedagogic way. The book should be read by all managers and leaders in service organizations with an interest in understanding the prerequisites for cost-effective service excellence.

Professor Bo Edvardsson, Director, Service Research Center – CTF; and editor of the *International Journal of Service Industry Management*

How is it possible that Singapore Airlines (SIA) is very successful in pursuing seemingly incompatible strategies? On the one hand, the company is a quality leader; on the other hand, it is able to produce its excellent services so efficiently that it is highly profitable. Loizos Heracleous, Jochen Wirtz and Nitin Pangarkar answer this intriguing question in a very impressive way. Their book is much more than just a best-practice description. It convinces through an excellent and systematic diagnostic analysis. The essential and self-reinforcing components of a 'cost-effective service excellence' are identified precisely. Besides, it is pointed out exactly which general lessons can be learned from SIA. The authors don't give quick 'how to'-recommendations. Instead, they succeed in brilliantly showing which questions need to be answered for a company to be successful in tough markets. This book is a 'must' for all ambitious managers who want to compare themselves with the best.

Professor Bernd Stauss, Chair of Services Management, Ingolstadt School of Management, Germany

Since 1990 I have flown more than one million miles on Singapore Airlines. The quality of service is consistently outstanding. Where else can you find such warm, professional, and responsive service in a brutally challenging industry? Singapore Airlines knows the secrets to delivering spectacular service and superior profits. Finally, this book reveals the inside secrets of 'cost-effective service excellence'. Great reading, great service!

Ron Kaufman, bestselling author, *UP Your Service!*®

There is probably no disputing the statement that the Singapore Airlines brand name is associated primarily with service excellence and a deep customer focus. In telling the Singapore Airlines story, this book goes under the surface to give the reader insights into how and why the company uses service excellence as a strategic lever, and more importantly how they execute this strategy at various customer touch points. While the story is told from the Singapore Airlines perspective, its lessons and intriguing insights ring loud for any service provider in any industry vertical.

Professor Dilip Soman, Corus Professor of Strategy and Professor of Marketing, Rotman School of Management, University of Toronto

Very refreshing … A strategic, analytical and yet pragmatic insight into how a world-class service organization translates a complex multi-faceted strategy into a clear, effective success story. A must read for senior management and entrepreneurs.

Nolan H.B. Tan, Chief Executive, Service Quality (SQ) Centre, Singapore

Managers who so far have kept a black bottom line through productivity gains experience that this route is running out on date. Being able to learn how Singapore Airlines managed to make healthy profits year in and out despite hyper-competition will be a welcoming reading. In this book, Heracleous, Wirtz and Pangarkar document and describe the five pillars of Singapore's service delivery system which offers unique value to its customers. It is my prediction that managers capable of developing a core competence of cost-effective service excellence and the cultural values to support it will be the winners in the new decade. While the recipe is simple its execution is hard. This book will provide you with a jumpstart in the race.

Tor W. Andreassen, Professor of Marketing, Norwegian School of Management

This book delivers an independent and detailed assessment of one of the world's best service organizations. Using a blend of theory and practice the authors provide a deep insight into the reasons for the success of SIA. The questions at the end of the chapters challenge the readers to apply the learning in their own organizations.

Professor Robert Johnston, Warwick Business School

This is a thoughtful book describing and analyzing the success story of a corporate icon in Singapore. It reveals a spectrum of hidden business practices that cause travellers to feel so good that they have chosen to fly with SIA. And it is also a treasure chest of trade secrets of how to build a great company. What an exciting read! I recommend it to all high-flying executives.

Dr Tan Tay Keong, Executive Director, Singapore International Foundation

In their lucid and insightful account of what makes Singapore Airlines such a distinctive company, Heracleous, Wirtz and Pangarkar offer a salutory reminder that there are no such things as industries that are 'good' or 'bad' or economic sectors that are 'old' or 'new'. At best such characterizations are oversimplifications of the basic economic structures of an industry. In contrast, the story of Singapore Airlines adds further proof to the thesis that what ultimately matters is whether companies can marshall their resources effectively and efficiently to create value for their shareholders, their customers and their employees. The 'non-secret' of success: A clear strategy realized through seamless execution. As a former management consultant and management practitioner in a 'very old economy' sector, I commend this practical, no-nonsense book.

Stavros Yiannouka, Vice-Dean, Lee Kuan Yew School of Public Policy and former senior consultant with McKinsey & Company

In the rough and tumble world of cutthroat airline competition, one company stands out as the undisputed global leader in almost every measurable category of performance year after year. That company is Singapore Airlines and this exceptional book tells you the story of exactly how they do it. The last chapter, summarizing strategic insights and lessons learned, is both an invaluable guide to managers seeking to benchmark the 'best of the best', as well as a major contribution to thinking about business strategy, execution and performance excellence.

Robert J. Marshak, Ph.D., Adjunct Professor-in-Residence, American University, Washington, DC, USA; and Associate Editor of the *Journal of Applied Behavioral Science*

Flying High in a Competitive Industry

◆

Cost-Effective Service Excellence at Singapore Airlines

Loizos Heracleous
Jochen Wirtz
Nitin Pangarkar

Singapore • Boston • Burr Ridge, IL • Dubuque, IA • Madison, WI
New York • San Francisco • St. Louis • Bangkok • Bogotá • Caracas
Kuala Lumpur • Lisbon • London • Madrid • Mexico City • Milan
Montreal • New Delhi • Santiago • Seoul • Sydney • Taipei • Toronto

The *McGraw-Hill* Companies

Flying High in a Competitive Industry
Cost-Effective Service Excellence at Singapore Airlines

 **Education**

Photos on pages xxiv, 56, 80, 116, 144 and 174 are used with permission from Singapore Airlines.

1 2 3 4 5 6 7 8 9 10 SSP BJE 09 08 07 06

When ordering this title, use ISBN 007-124964-8

Printed in Singapore

To Fiona, the light of my life

Loizos Heracleous

To Jeannette and our children, Lorraine, Stefanie and Alexander, with love

Jochen Wirtz

To Ashwini and our children, Natasha and Anish, with love

Nitin Pangarkar

Contents

CONTENTS

Preface

This book aims to answer a simple but intriguing question: How has Singapore Airlines (SIA) managed to make healthy profits year in year out, in an industry whose performance over the years has been dismal? SIA's profitability has been exceptional, superior in the long term to that of the competitors in its peer group. By answering this question, through our in-depth research on the airline industry and SIA, we derive some general lessons for managers in other industries.

We begin the book with an analysis of the airline industry and its key trends, moving on to a broad outline of SIA's strategic drivers of success. We then focus on specific elements of

SIA's strategy and organization, such as its core competency of cost-effective service excellence, its innovation capabilities and its human resource management practices. We end with some strategic lessons that we believe apply to any organization that aims to achieve sustainable success in hyper-competitive markets.

Chapter 1 analyses the airline industry as a whole, reviewing its historical development, important trends over time and key aspects of the industry's economics. Issues discussed include the impact of government intervention; uncontrollable factors such as oil prices and political events; factors such as the perishability of seats, seasonality of demand, and long time horizons in infrastructural decisions that inject additional levels of complexity; airlines' fixed and variable direct operating costs and their indirect operating costs; and lastly the chronically poor and volatile performance of the whole industry. Key trends in the industry, such as the formation of alliances and the emergence of budget carriers, are examined. Lastly, strategic imperatives for airlines are considered, such as adopting cutting-edge technology, controlling costs and raising productivity, managing alliances effectively, avoiding the herd instinct, and overcoming commoditization.

Chapter 2 then focuses on SIA itself, looking at its impor-tant strategic choices and resource deployment decisions, in order to get a broad understanding of the company's superior performance. Factors discussed include its young fleet, low staff costs, global revenue base, striving for efficiency, brand reputation, response to crises, and alliance and acquisition strategies. In addition to their significant individual impacts on SIA's performance, these factors also interact with one another, thus enhancing the magnitude of their impacts. A key conclusion drawn from this analysis is that SIA's superior performance is attributable to a complex array of strategic decisions which have been highly consistent over time.

Chapter 3 addresses what we believe is SIA's core competence: cost-effective service excellence. It is relatively easy to deliver excellent service if one pours money into doing so. What is much harder to do is to deliver service excellence in an efficient manner, in other words implementing a strategy that integrates differentiation and cost leadership. How has SIA managed to achieve this? In common with other organizations with a reputation for service excellence, SIA displays characteristics such as top management commitment, customer-focused staff and systems, and a customer-oriented culture. However, our research has provided further insights into how SIA develops and maintains a reputation for service excellence, which its achieves through what we call the 'five pillars' of SIA's activity system. These pillars are rigorous service design and development, total innovation, profit and cost consciousness ingrained in all employees, holistic staff development, and reaping of strategic synergies through related diversification and world-class infrastructure. These five pillars of SIA's cost-effective service excellence are supported, operationalized, and made real to everyday decisions and actions through a self-reinforcing activity system of virtuous circles, presented in the chapter. The core competence of cost-effective service excellence, and the cultural values supporting it, are ingrained into both the hearts and minds of employees as well as into organizational processes. This may help explain why SIA's competitive advantage has been sustained for decades. While it is easy to copy single elements, it is much harder to reproduce an entire, self-reinforcing, activity system.

The chapter proceeds to discuss SIA's investments in biometrics, further illustrating the two pillars of rigorous service design and development as well as total innovation. SIA has started to employ biometric technologies to enhance the customer experience while at the same time raising security and efficiency. We suggest that sustaining competitive advantage through the strategic use of technology involves developing innovations that have a significant positive impact on the customer experience and also entails significant business process redesign to make the processes difficult to imitate.

Chapter 4 continues the theme of service excellence with a focus on innovation. It sheds light on SIA's ability to be a serial innovator, introducing many firsts in the airline industry and sustaining this innovative orientation over decades in the face of intense cost pressures, industry crises and the push towards commoditization. We first present senior management's perspective of the key challenges they face in delivering sustained and cost-effective service excellence. These challenges include, firstly, how to consistently satisfy the sky-high and rising expectations of customers; secondly, how to deal effectively with the tension arising from offering uniform service that is at the same time personalized; and, thirdly, how to approach a large number of services in a holistic manner to attain consistent excellence in all related processes and subprocesses.

The chapter proceeds to address SIA's innovation process, characterized by the seamless combination of hard, structured and rigorous innovation that is centralized with soft, emergent and continuous innovation that is undertaken by different functional departments. This competence is further enhanced through an integrated customer and front-line staff feedback system that provides valuable insights on innovation.

Chapter 5 then addresses SIA's human resource management processes, a crucial aspect of any service business, where people, especially front-line staff, are a core part of the offering and the most visible element of the service. The chapter analyzes the five elements forming SIA's human resource management and how each of these elements reinforces its service excellence strategy. The five elements are stringent selection and hiring of people, extensive training and retraining, formation of successful service delivery teams, empowerment of the front line, and staff motivation. Even though these service elements are simple to state, very few firms have been able to implement systems that deliver the desired results.

The reason we undertook this study was to gain a deeper understanding of the factors that can help a company achieve sustainable success in extremely tough industries, based on a detailed study of the strategy and the organizational features of a company that has achieved just that. Chapter 6 presents some lessons from our research into SIA, which we believe apply to any company that aims to achieve sustainable competitive advantage, the holy grail of strategy. We do not aim to provide the answers but rather to suggest useful strategic principles and to help executives ask the right questions. The chapter begins by reminding us why it is so hard to be successful in the airline industry. We then proceed with strategic lessons, which relate to the need to be clear about the company's generic strategy (or a combination of generic strategies); the need to achieve high levels of strategic alignment among strategy, capabilities, organization and market demands; the importance of nurturing and investing in capabilities and core competencies that support the strategy; and finally the need to understand and foster strategic innovation. We then examine SIA's institutional context and suggest that, even though SIA has definitely gained from being located in a supportive institutional context, this is far from a comprehensive explanation of its success. Its success can ultimately be traced to robust strategies, seamless execution, and continuous vigilance and realignment.

Our research started in 2001 to examine SIA's strategy and competitiveness over the years, in particular its competencies of service excellence, efficiency and innovation. We have conducted both primary and secondary data gathering on these themes. In addition to researching library and database resources on the airline industry and on SIA, we have up to the time of writing this book, conducted a total of 16 in-depth interviews with a view to gaining a deeper appreciation of how SIA has managed to achieve sustainable competitive advantage and outperform all other airlines in its peer group for decades.

We are grateful to all the people at SIA who kindly allowed us to interview them to gain a deeper understanding of what makes SIA tick. They include, in alphabetical order, Mr Choo Poh Leong, Mr Timothy Chua, Dr Goh Ban Eng, Ms Lam Seet Mui, Ms Lim Suu Kuan, Mr Sim Kay Wee, Mr Toh Giam Ming, Ms Betty Wong, Mr Yap Kim Wah and Dr Yeoh Teng Kwong. We would also like to thank Ms Karen Liaw and Ms Roshini

Prakash of SIA's public affairs office, who were instrumental in helping us arrange the interviews at SIA. We are thankful to the people at the Civil Aviation Authority of Singapore who gave us insights into the development of the biometrics project, in particular Mr Poh Young Peng and Mr Wang Pei Chong. Furthermore, we are indebted to Professor Robert Johnston at Warwick Business School, who has collaborated with us on a number of research projects involving SIA, and to Professor Christopher Lovelock at Yale University who has collaborated with Jochen on a number of services marketing books that provided the conceptual underpinning of Chapter 5. We thank our research assistants Arnab Banerjee, Patricia Chew, Nikhil Kochhar, Lou Seng Lee, Canice Liu, Ravi Prakash, Ritesh Toshniwal and Dai Ziyun for helping with data gathering and preparation of figures. We thank our publisher, McGraw-Hill, in particular Ms Pauline Chua. Lastly, we express our gratitude to our families for putting up with the countless hours we spent in front of the computer working on this book.

The Authors

As a team, Loizos Heracleous, Jochen Wirtz and Nitin Pangarkar, possess a unique blend of skills and experience that is ideally suited to writing a definite, illustrative and engaging book on cost-effective service excellence set in a highly competitive industry.

 **Loizos Heracleous** is an Official Fellow of Templeton College, Oxford University, specializing in strategy and organization. He lived and worked in Asia for eight years, in his previous post as associ-

ate professor of corporate strategy at the National University of Singapore. Loizos earned his Ph.D. at the Judge Institute of Management Studies, University of Cambridge. He is the author of *Strategy and Organization: Realizing Strategic Management* (2003); *Discourse, Interpretation, Organization* (2006); and co-author of *Business Strategy in Asia: A Casebook* (2004).

Loizos is a Senior Editor of *Organization Studies*, and serves on the editorial boards of the *Journal of Applied Behavioral Science*, *Journal of Management Studies* and *Asia Pacific Journal of Management*. He has published over 40 research papers in international journals, including the *Academy of Management Journal*, *Harvard Business Review*, *MIT Sloan Management Review*, *Journal of Management Studies*, *Human Relations*, and *Journal of Applied Behavioral Science*. His research was honoured by two *Best Paper Awards* from the US Academy of Management, in 1999 and 2004.

In addition to Cyprus where he was born, Loizos has lived and worked in the UK, Ireland, Hong Kong and Singapore; and travelled extensively around the world. He has developed and conducted several executive development programmes in areas such as strategic thinking and planning, corporate governance, corporate social responsibility, diagnosing and managing organizational culture, managing transformational change, and organizing for the future. He trained company directors in Singapore on corporate governance on behalf of the Singapore Institute of Directors from 1999–2004. He has also trained executives and advised several organizations in areas related to strategy, organization and leadership. Loizos has been listed in the Marquis Who's Who in the World since 2003.

 **Jochen Wirtz** is one of the leading authorities in services marketing in Asia. He is an Associate Professor of Marketing at the National University of Singapore, where he teaches services marketing in MBA and executive programmes. He is also the co-director of the UCLA–NUS Executive MBA Programme, NUS's dual degree programme with UCLA.

Dr Wirtz's recent book *Services Marketing – People, Technology, Strategy* (2004), co-authored with Professor Christopher Lovelock, is one of the top two services marketing text books globally, and his co-authored book *Services Marketing in Asia-People* (2005) has become the leading services marketing text in Asia. His research focuses on service management and he has published some 50 academic articles in, among others, *Harvard Business Review, Journal of Business Research, Journal of Consumer Psychology, Journal of Retailing, Journal of the Academy of Marketing Science, Journal of Services Marketing, Journal of Service Research, Managing Service Quality* and *Psychology and Marketing*. He has also published over 70 conference papers, 8 books and more than 40 book chapters. Dr Wirtz is on the editorial boards of seven journals, and has received a dozen research and teaching awards, including the Emerald Literati Club 2003 Award for Excellence for the most outstanding paper of the year in the *International Journal of Service Industry Management*, and the prestigious university-wide Outstanding Educator Award at the National University of Singapore. Dr Wirtz is also active as a management consultant, working with both international consulting firms including Accenture,

Arthur D. Little and KPMG, and major service companies in the areas of strategy, business development and service management across Asia.

Dr Wirtz received his Ph.D. in services marketing from the London Business School, and holds a BA (Hons) in marketing and accounting and a professional certification in banking from Germany. Originally from Germany, Dr Wirtz moved to Asia in 1992 after studying and working in London for seven years.

 **Nitin Pangarkar** is Associate Professor of Business Policy at the NUS Business School. Previously, he held academic positions at the University of Minnesota (USA) and the Helsinki School of Economics (Finland). His research interests lie in the areas of strategic management and international business – specifically cross-border strategic alliances and global strategy. Dr Pangarkar's research has been presented in several international conferences around the world and published in the form of more than 30 international journal articles, conference proceedings, cases and book chapters. He is a member of several professional organizations and serves as the secretary of the *Asia Academy of Management*, the leading regional association for management scholars in Asia. He also serves on the editorial boards of two international journals.

Dr Pangarkar is a co-author of *Business Strategy in Asia: A casebook* (2001 and 2004). The book has been translated into Mandarin and the cumulative sales of the book has exceeded 14,000 copies. Dr Pangarkar's teaching and case materials have been used in many universities around the world including MIT, the Chinese University of Hong Kong, Macquarie University, the University of Western Australia, Copenhagen Business School and Nanyang Technological University. He has taught in several executive development programmes at NUS and has also been an invited speaker for several managerial conferences. He has been quoted in reputed newspapers and publications including the *International Herald Tribune*, *The Edge* (Malaysia), *Today* (Singapore) and the *Economics Times* (India). He is a recipient of several awards including the Outstanding Educator Award and the Outstanding Service Award from the NUS Business School and the Excellent Teacher Award from the National University of Singapore. Dr Pangarkar has also served as a strategy consultant to many organizations including Bekaert (Belgium/China) and IE Singapore, among others.

1

The Airline Industry: Trends, Economics, Performance and Strategic Imperatives

The airline industry, one of the most visible sectors of a nation's infrastructure, has enormous economic significance. In 2003, the world's 896 scheduled airlines carried 1.657 billion passengers – equivalent to more than 25% of the earth's inhabitants – and 34.5 million tonnes of freight. The industry also carried almost 40% (by value) of the world's manufactured exports and 45% of the more than 714 million international tourists (2002 data).[1] It is expected to assume even greater importance over the coming years, especially in transporting freight, accounting for as much as 80% by value of the world's freight by 2014.

According to estimates by the International Civil Aviation Organization (ICAO), the direct contribution of civil aviation (including airlines, other commercial air transport operators and their affiliates) was US$370 billion in 1998. Civil aviation makes an even larger contribution to the gross domestic product of developed countries such as the United States, where air travel forms an important part of business and personal lives.[2] The sector is also becoming increasingly important for the residents of developing countries as air travel becomes more affordable.

The civil aviation industry also has a multiplier effect which goes well beyond its direct contribution, spanning industries that have some interdependence with aviation (e.g., travel agencies and the range of businesses associated with air freight). Considering the direct and multiplier effects of air transport, a total US$1,360 billion of output and 27.2 million jobs were generated worldwide in 1998. In terms of employment, the sector accounted for almost 6 million jobs, with 2.3 million people directly employed by airlines and the remaining 3.7 million employed by closely related sectors such as air navigation service providers (1.9 million) as well as aircraft and other manufacturers (1.8 million).

For much of the last 30 years, the airline industry has simultaneously experienced falling yields (the sector's equivalent of prices) and increasing overall revenues, implying a greater volume in terms of trips undertaken by customers and the amount of freight handled. Even during the ten years leading up to 2003, when the decline in yields was the most significant (owing to widespread liberalization of the sector and the entry of scores of new players), the sector was able to raise its total revenues by 28% (see Figure 1–1). Between 1991 and 2002, the scheduled airlines' traffic increased at an annual rate of 4.9%, a composite of passenger-kilometres, which grew at 4.3%, and freight tonne-kilometres, which grew at 6.5%.

Figure 1–1
Operating revenues of the airline sector

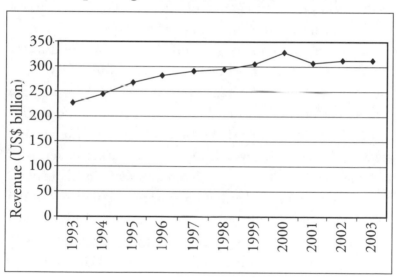

Sources: *ICAO Journal,* no. 6 (1996, 2004).

This chapter will examine the economies, the trends and the strategic imperatives of the airline industry. But first we will look at the evolution of the industry.

Historical Development

The first scheduled airline flight took off in 1912. During the first 30 years of development, the technology underlying the aircraft (which was based on the piston engine), placed severe constraints on the growth of the industry owing to several factors: low speed, low level of comfort, short range (distance) and low cost-effectiveness. During the 1950s, aircraft powered by turboprop engines were introduced, which dramatically improved the productivity and production capacity of the industry (see Table 1–1). An even bigger technological advance, in the form of the jet engine, occurred in the 1960s, and it boosted the further development of the industry.

Air travel was a luxury in many parts of the world in the past decades and, as a result, domestic travel within developed countries, such as the United States, formed by far the largest component of the industry. While the US domestic market continues to dwarf other domestic markets (e.g., the Japanese market is about one-seventh of the US market in terms of passengers),[3] over the last two decades, international air travel has increased in many developing countries (especially in Asia Pacific) as their citizens become more affluent. This trend is evident from the following figures. Between 1980 and 1999, the growth in international revenue passenger-kilometres[4] and the number of international passengers was more than twice the growth in the world's gross domestic product (about 3%) and much faster than the growth in the overall number of passengers. As recently as 1991, airlines in North America and Europe accounted for 71.1% of the worldwide traffic, but this proportion had declined to 63% by 2002. Over the same period,

Table 1-1
Evolution of aircraft technology

Period	Most productive model (technology)*	Year of introduction	Number of seats	Hourly productivity (tonne-km/h)[†]	Annual production capacity (thousand tonne-km)
1930s–40s	DC-3 (piston)	1936	21	527	1,571
1950s	Britannia 310 (turboprop)	1956	139	6,048	18,144
1960s	Boeing 720B	1960	149 (single class)	11,256	33,770
	Boeing 747 (turbojet)	1969	550	31,935	95,805
1980s	Boeing 747–400	1989	568	44,350	133,050
2000s	Airbus A380	2005	882	52,500	Not available

Sources: Compiled based on data from Doganis (1991, 2001).

* Several other aircraft models not mentioned in the table (e.g., Concorde, Boeing 777 and short-haul Airbus planes such as A300 and A320) have lower levels of productivity than the most productive model.

[†] Tonne-km/h is arrived at by simply multiplying the capacity of the plane (in tonnes) by the speed of travel (in kilometres per hour).

airlines from Asia Pacific increased their share from 19.5% to 26.7%. The growth of airlines based in Asia Pacific has been phenomenal (see Figure 1–2). Between 1978 and 1988, they witnessed an annual growth of 10.4% (based on tonne-kilometres) in their international operations and 7.6% in domestic operations. Moreover, the International Air Transport Association (IATA) forecasts that the Asia Pacific market will account for 51% of the scheduled international passengers in 2010.[5]

These trends, specifically the rising importance of international travel and Asia Pacific markets, are expected to continue, perhaps even accelerate, owing to three key factors.[6] First, continued strong performance of Asia Pacific economies will translate into a higher number of trips on a per capita basis for both business and leisure purposes. The low base (e.g., in India and China, only one person in every 100 might take a flight during a year) means the region has a huge potential for growth. Secondly, demographics indicate that urbanization, a key predictor of the demand for air travel, is occurring rapidly in Asia Pacific economies.[7] Thirdly, many of these economies are exhibiting rapid population growth, in contrast to the slow or negative growth in many developed countries, especially Europe and Japan.

Industry Economics

Government intervention

The airline industry is characterized by an unusually high degree of government intervention, especially for international air

Figure 1–2
Passenger and freight traffic in different regions (2002)

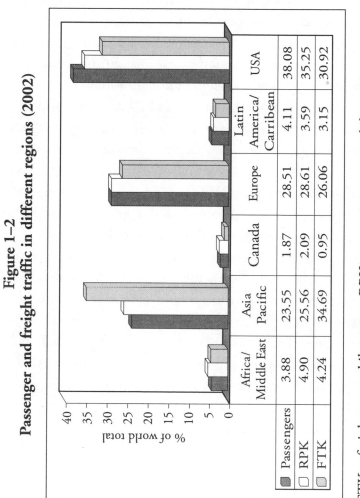

	Africa/ Middle East	Asia Pacific	Canada	Europe	Latin America/ Carribean	USA
Passengers	3.88	23.55	1.87	28.51	4.11	38.08
RPK	4.90	25.56	2.09	28.61	3.59	35.25
FTK	4.24	34.69	0.95	26.06	3.15	30.92

FTK = freight tonne-kilometres, RPK = revenue passenger-kilometres.
Source: 'Battered and bruised', *Air Transport World*, July 2003, pp. 29–30.

routes. The motivations behind government intervention include national pride, the strategic importance of the sector and the safety of passengers. As a starting basis for intervention, many governments (at least historically) believed that having a national carrier (the flag carrier) was a matter of national pride. Consequently, they started national airlines. Additionally, many governments consider air transport to be essential for the functioning of the country and its economy, and even a matter of national security. Finally, since a single aircraft may carry several hundred passengers, whose safety may be jeopardized by inappropriate airline policies, poor maintenance and safety standards, it is necessary for government agencies (such as the US Federal Aviation Administration) to stipulate safety standards and also oversee compliance by airlines.

Government intervention in the airline sector takes several different forms. With the notable exception of countries that have signed open skies agreements with each other, airlines have to obtain approval from the home and host governments for the international routes served and the flight frequency. In fact, an elaborate categorization of freedoms determines what a particular airline can or cannot do in a foreign market (see Table 1–2).

Constraints on flight routes and/or frequency are used by governments to protect their domestic airlines, as illustrated by the following cases:

Only three airlines are permitted to operate flights on the busy Hong Kong–London Heathrow route, and they are Cathay Pacific, British Airways and Virgin Atlantic.

Table 1–2
Regulation of air traffic

Freedom	Implication
First	The right of an airline of one country to fly over the territory of another country without landing.
Second	The right of an airline of one country to land in another country for non-traffic reasons, such as maintenance or refuelling, while en-route to another country.
Third	The right of an airline of one country to carry traffic from its country of registry to another country.
Fourth	The right of an airline of one country to carry traffic from another country to its own country of registry.
Fifth	The right of an airline of one country to carry traffic between two countries outside of its own country of registry as long as the flight originates or terminates in its own country of registry.
Sixth	The right of an airline of one country to carry traffic between foreign countries via its own country of registry. This is a combination of the third and fourth freedoms.
Seventh	The right of an airline of one country to operate stand-alone services entirely outside the territory of its home country to carry traffic between two foreign countries.
Eight	The right of an airline of one country to carry traffic between two points within the territory of a foreign country (cabotage).

Source: Button et al. (1998), p. 31.

As of February 2005, while Singapore Airlines (SIA) flies as many as 80 times a week from Singapore to Australia, all its flights have to terminate in Australia and cannot proceed to the United States. Qantas, which has a 75% market share of the Australia–US routes and derives 41% of its international profits from these routes, is strongly opposed to SIA obtaining these flying rights.[8]

Leaving aside issues of allowing full foreign ownership, governments often place restrictions on foreign investors taking equity stakes in their countries' airlines. For instance, non-US investors cannot own more than 25% of a US airline's voting stock, while the limit is 31% in Canada, and 49% in the European Union. Such restrictions prevented AMR Corporation (the parent of American Airlines) from bailing out the financially strapped Canadian Airlines by a Quebec judge, on the basis that it violated Canada's foreign ownership limit.[9] These restrictions limit the possibility of international expansion for even the most efficient and best-managed airlines (e.g., SIA and Emirates) and lead to dependence on alliances to overcome these constraints.

In the past, many governments also intervened by subsidizing loss-making airlines. The commission approved state aid to eight European airlines was reported to amount to an average of US$1.511 billion for the 1990–97 period. Such aid distorts market forces (e.g., excess capacity persists as a result), makes the playing field uneven and puts pressure on healthy airlines. In recent years, governments have increasingly shown reluctance to shore up financially struggling airlines. Belgium, for instance, did not choose to save the struggling Sabena through subsidies. The airline, instead, was bought by Swissair prior to the latter's bankruptcy. In another instance, in the aftermath of the 11 September 2001 air attacks on the United States, when airlines worldwide suffered huge losses, no government in Latin America gave financial support to its national carrier.[10]

Over the last two decades, the degree of government intervention in civil aviation has declined substantially. As a first sign, governments are becoming more open to divesting their stake in airlines. Between 1985 and 2003, some 130 countries announced privatization plans or expressed their intention to privatize about 190 nationally owned airlines. The plans were not always followed by action, however, and by end 2000 only 62 carriers had been privatized, 37 of them since 1995. Some governments (e.g., Malaysia and New Zealand) have even gone in the opposite direction, buying back their national airlines after privatizing them.[11]

The trend of deregulation has spilled over into the control of routes. The United States pioneered deregulation of the airline industry in 1978, and its lead was followed by Europe starting in 1989 and implemented on a broader scale in 1997. Most Asian countries, with the notable exception of a few countries such as Singapore, are lagging behind in this respect. On a bilateral basis, many governments have signed open skies agreements, which give complete freedom to their countries' carriers to choose their routes and frequency of flights to the signatory countries.

CHAPTER 1

❖ ❖ ❖

Managing the uncontrollables

The airline industry is also atypical in the sense that it is impacted by several factors beyond its control. Besides government intervention, these factors include oil prices, airport and other charges, the quality of infrastructure, and political and other events which affect the financial health of the industry (see Figure 1–3).

Oil, which forms one of the most important inputs for an airline, is a globally traded commodity whose price is determined by market demand and supply (see Figure 1–4). Furthermore, oil price is denominated in US dollars, while many international airlines earn a substantial portion of their revenues in local currencies (e.g., Qantas in Australian dollars). Consequently, many international airlines bear a significant foreign exchange risk.[12] While fuel costs account for a smaller proportion of total costs today than 20 years ago, sharp upswings in oil prices, nevertheless, impact the bottom line of airlines. United Airlines, for instance, incurred a US$75 million operating loss for April 2004 as a result of unusually high fuel prices, which constituted its second largest category of expenses, behind labour. Even Southwest Airlines, an efficiently managed and well-performing airline, was forced to offer buyout packages to its non-executive employees as a belt-tightening measure in response to high oil prices.[13]

Governments and airports impose charges such as landing and aircraft parking fees, which are sometimes quite different from prevailing market prices. Although oil is a globally traded commodity, there is significant variation in

Figure 1–3
Determinants of airline profitability

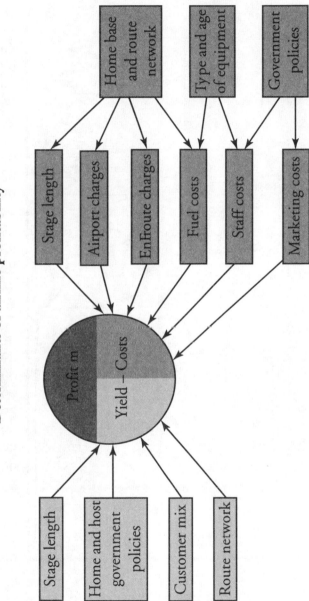

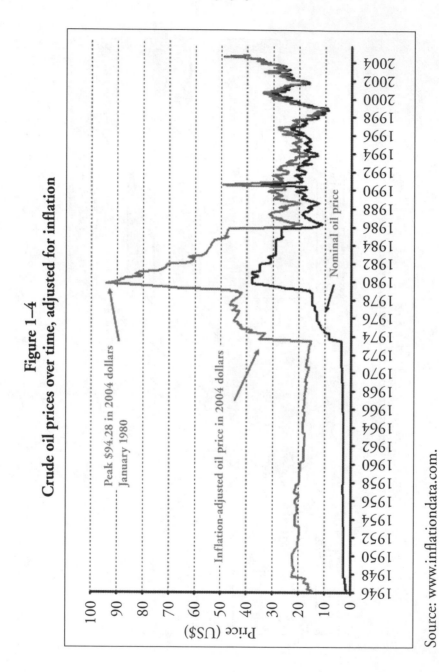

Figure 1–4
Crude oil prices over time, adjusted for inflation

Source: www.inflationdata.com.

the price of jet fuel across the world, again due to local factors and policies. Airlines must take these fees and prices (which may be quite independent of true market prices) as 'given', without any possibility of negotiations. EasyJet, a budget carrier founded by Greek shipping tycoon Stelios Haji-Ioannou, pulled out of Zurich Airport in protest of the airport charging what the airline believed were unreasonable fees for landing and other support services, and it warned that it would pull out of other airports if the rates were not kept at sensible levels.[14]

Issues such as the quality of the local infrastructure, which is the responsibility of the government, also critically affect the growth and profitability of airlines. The US government readily admits that the air traffic system in the country is based on 1960s technology and operating concepts and is close to gridlock because of the rapid increase in traffic – 40% in 1991 itself.[15] In Scandinavia and India, inappropriate government policies have held back the development of airlines. Air travel in India is only available to the residents of large and medium-sized cities leaving gaping holes in coverage. It is also expensive, regulatory barriers having propped up inefficient carriers, and offers generally low convenience, especially in terms of flight frequency and punctuality. Another issue is that airport infrastructure may be inadequate to accommodate the new generation of jumbo jets. For example, the deployment of the latest Airbus A380 aircraft will require airports to modify runways.

Airlines are also affected by political and other events that might influence travel and tourism. The Gulf war in 1991 caused air traffic to decline for the first time in aviation history. By 1992, a combination of lower traffic, excess capacity and high oil prices led to huge losses in earnings for airlines that exceeded all the profits earned by the industry in its 67-year history.[16] In recent years, political and other events have assumed greater importance as a result of a series of far-reaching events including the 11 September terrorist attacks, the wars in Afghanistan and Iraq, and the outbreak of the severe acute respiratory syndrome (SARS). While the impact of the crises themselves is quite visible in terms of reduced demand for travel for the duration of the crisis, there are second-order, less visible effects that impact the airline industry, even after the event. For instance, after the 11 September hijackings, the added security procedures put in place have increased the time passengers spent in pre-flight procedures. Many airports and governments have also imposed new taxes to cover the cost of these additional procedures, which can raise airfares (especially for short-haul routes or for budget airlines) by as much as 20%.[17] Both these factors have affected the demand for air travel, especially at the margin where air travel is discretionary (e.g., for leisure) or may be substituted by alternatives (e.g., cars or trains for price-sensitive customers and private jets for high-end business travellers).

Complexity

A number of factors on the demand side, such as the perishable nature of seats on a particular flight, the high level of seasonality as well as cyclicality, and the exceptionally long time horizon for making important decisions such as aircraft acquisition, all increase the complexity of managing airlines.

Airline service, specifically a seat on a particular flight and on a given day, is perishable and cannot be inventoried. While airlines have devised a variety of price discrimination strategies (e.g., by offering a wide array of fares on a given flight) to address the perishability issue, sometimes they have shown a tendency to engage in destructive price competition while trying to fill seats.

Demand for air travel is cyclical as well as seasonal. While seasonality is easy to anticipate (e.g., peak travel during holiday periods), it is difficult to address since catering to peak demand will lead to excess capacity during other times. On the other hand, not maintaining excess capacity will lead to lost revenues during the peak seasons. According to an industry expert, the industry can be considered as operating at full capacity at a utilization rate of 70%–75%.[18]

Cyclical demand poses even greater challenges to airline executives. During the trough of the business cycle, the high fixed costs adversely affect financial performance. The peak of the business cycle, on the other hand, often induces executives to overextend their company by ordering new planes, hiring more employees or promising generous pay packages to attract and retain employees, all of which might prove unsustainable in other stages of the cycle.

Airline executives also face the difficult task of planning for exceptionally long time horizons, especially relating to aircraft procurement. A large jet aircraft costs in excess of US$200 million, and its procurement typically involves significant lead time. Since an aircraft has an operating life of 25–30 years, airline executives may be committing themselves to a period of 30 years or more while placing a new aircraft order.[19] Assumptions regarding the regulatory, economic or operating environments can easily go awry over such a long time and adversely affect the airline's performance. If an airline uses debt financing to purchase aircraft, it is exposed to even greater risk in the event the environment turns unfavourable.

Cost structure of airlines

Broadly, airline operating costs can be grouped into three categories:[20]

- Variable direct operating costs. These are activity or flight related and are escapable in the short term. They include fuel costs, variable flight crew costs (e.g., allowances), direct engineering costs (related to, for instance, the number of flying cycles or hours), airport and en-route charges, and passenger service costs (e.g., meals).
- Fixed direct operating costs. These are fleet-size related and are escapable in the medium term. They include aircraft depreciation or rental, annual flight crew costs (fixed salaries unrelated to the number of flying hours), annual cabin crew costs (fixed salaries), and engineering overheads (e.g., fixed engineering costs unrelated to aircraft utilization).

- Indirect operating costs. These are route or product related and are escapable in the medium to long term. They include station and ground expenses, passenger service expenses (e.g., passenger service staff costs, passenger insurance), expenses related to ticketing sales and promotions and general and administrative expenses.

While the cost structure (the proportion of total costs accounted by each of these categories) varies across airlines, the following issues are common to all airlines. First, operating costs vary by the route structure owing to significant variation in local charges (landing, parking, en-route, etc.) and costs such as jet fuel. Operating costs decline with longer stage length, providing a cost advantage to airlines that focus on long-haul routes. Secondly, the four largest categories of costs are labour, fuel, aircraft acquisitions, and maintenance and repair. In developed countries, labour costs constitute the largest portion of an airline's costs, sometimes amounting to as much as 35%–40% (see Figure 1–5 for the cost structure of US airlines). Airlines from developing countries enjoy an advantage in this respect, since their wages and social costs are lower. Finally, a significant portion (75% according to some estimates) of an airline's costs is fixed, independent of whether a particular flight is operated or not on a given day or the number of passengers on a particular flight.[21] Since the marginal costs of carrying an additional passenger are low, airlines tend to be overzealous in discounting prices leading to fluctuating revenues and profits (due to high fixed costs).

Figure 1–5
US airlines' cost components

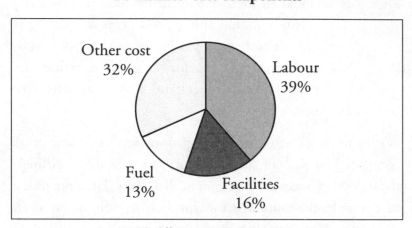

(a) All cost components

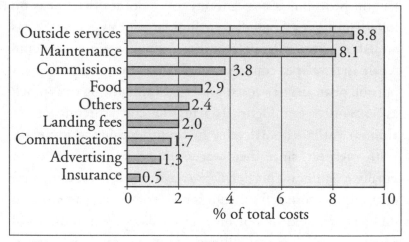

(b) Components of other costs

Source: Taneja (2003).

Performance

While commercial aviation enjoys a prominent role in the world economy and has experienced a healthy growth over the last few decades, industry participants have faced significant challenges in attaining consistent levels of profitability, as suggested by the following figures: Between 1947 and 2000, the airline industry attained a net profit margin of less than 1%, making it a low performer compared to most other industries. During the 1945–93 period, airlines suffered as many as 13 years of losses. Between 1969 and 1994,[22] US-based airlines achieved the average profit margin of the industry only once.

The difficulty in achieving profitability is summed by an industry executive: "When we first started flying, we launched an airplane to a destination in the hope that it would get there. A few years later, we launched an airplane in the hope that it would get there on time. Today, we launch an airplane and hope that it will make a dollar."[23] Adam Thomson, the charismatic founder of British Caledonian Airlines, was cited as saying, "Recession is when you tighten your belt. Depression is when you no longer have a belt to tighten. When you've lost your trousers, you're in the airline business."[24]

Over the years, there have been a few bright spots in the industry's financial performance, mostly coinciding with a combination of the following factors: significant technological advances (e.g., the introduction of jet transport in the 1960s), economic boom (e.g., the period between 1993 and 2000) or low fuel prices. Unfortunately, for the airline industry's participants, prosperity has often been followed by severe adversity attributable to broader economic conditions and/or high fuel prices (see Table 1–3 and Figure 1–6).

Falling passenger and freight yields represent a key factor for the low industry profitability. Passenger yield (the equivalent of prices for the industry) fell at an annualized rate of 2.2% for the period 1985–99 and 3% for 1990–99. Freight yield fell at an annualized rate of 3.2% and 2.8% for the same periods. According to one estimate, the real yield (i.e., prices adjusted

Table 1–3
Financial performance of the airline sector over time

Time period	Financial performance	Factors
1960–67	Good	Strong productivity gains resulted from the introduction of jet aircraft.
1967–74	Poor, with major losses	Excess capacity in the late 1960s, the first oil shock, poor political climate (e.g., Arab–Israel war) and the threat of terrorism dried up demand.
1975–78	Good	Falling fuel and other costs (on a real basis) and buoyant demand lifted results.
1979–83	Poor	Second oil shock and intense competition among airlines to fill seats led to bankruptcy of carriers such as Braniff and Laker.

Table 1–3 (continued)

Time period	Financial performance	Factors
1984–90	Good	Despite a few untoward events (e.g., American bombing of Libya, Chernobyl disaster), the world economy performed robustly. That, coupled with falling costs for many airlines, led to good results. But debt burdens were heavy for some carriers by the end of the period and were expected to worsen with almost 7,000 planes on order for delivery between 1990 and 2001.
1990–92	Poor, with major losses	Recession in many parts of the world coupled with the Gulf war and high oil prices led to losses.
1993–2000	Good, with strong profits	Booming world economy, low oil prices and interest rates, and political stability led to unprecedented profits.
2001–2003	Poor, with large losses	The 11 September terrorist attacks and the subsequent military conflicts, coupled with the hangover from the excess capacity in prior years, led to unprecedented losses with major carriers seeking bankruptcy protection (e.g., US Airways, United Airlines).

Sources: For 1967–90 data, Doganis (1991); for data after 1991, *ICAO Journal.*

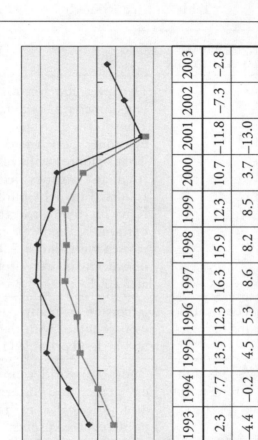
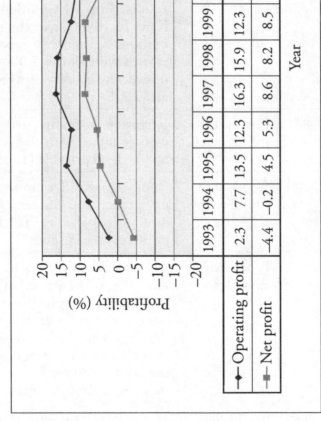

Figure 1–6
Profitability of airlines worldwide

	1993	1994	1995	1996	1997	1998	1999	2000	2001	2002	2003
Operating profit	2.3	7.7	13.5	12.3	16.3	15.9	12.3	10.7	−11.8	−7.3	−2.8
Net profit	−4.4	−0.2	4.5	5.3	8.6	8.2	8.5	3.7	−13.0		

Year

Profitability (%)

for inflation) fell from 12.5 US cents per revenue passenger-kilometre in 1970 to just over 6 cents in 2001.[25]

Though profitability has proved to be an elusive goal, airlines worldwide have succeeded, without doubt, in providing high levels of safety to their passengers. In fact, the diligence of airlines and effective oversight by governments have given the industry a far superior safety record compared with most other modes of transportation, especially cars. The odds of being killed on a single airline flight vary from 1 in 7.71 million to 1 in 558,000 for the top 25 airlines with the best safety records and the bottom 25 airlines with the worst safety records respectively. The odds of being on an airline flight which results in at least one fatality vary from 1 in 3.72 million to 1 in 419,000, again depending on whether a passenger is travelling on the top 25 airlines or the bottom 25.[26]

The airline industry has also succeeded in various other aspects including the following:

- Improving accessibility through high frequency of flights and far-reaching networks. The frequency of flights available between high-density markets (e.g., Boston–New York, Taipei–Hong Kong, Kuala Lumpur–Singapore) is especially remarkable.
- Attaining high reliability in terms of completed flights (in the high 90% range) and flights arriving on time despite uncontrollable factors such as the weather as well as airport and air-traffic control capacities.
- Providing affordable travel options through continuous improvement in technology (e.g., new generations of jets) and yield management systems.

- Introducing innovations especially for passengers travelling in higher service classes, who can now enjoy bed-like seats, a range of entertainment options and generally high service levels.

Recent Strategic Trends

Airline alliances

The concept of airline alliances is not new. IATA can be considered as a giant alliance set up by the world's leading airlines to coordinate international fares. Alliances were first seen in the US domestic market between major jet and commuter operators for the purpose of jointly developing the market (e.g., providing feeder services). Alliance activity, however, witnessed significant growth during the 1980s and 1990s as a response to the pressures of globalization. Faced with the twin requirements of building a global presence and achieving a more efficient cost structure, and yet constrained from undertaking mergers or starting new airlines in foreign markets, airlines found alliances to be a logical strategic alternative.

Alliance is a broad term which includes a variety of inter-firm cooperation and coordination ranging from formal cooperation through equity ownership in a partner to informal coordination through frequent flyer programmes.

Estimates of alliance activity vary across studies because, firstly, alliances are dynamic and airlines may be continually forming new ones as well as disbanding old ones. Secondly, the definition of alliances varies. The *Airline Business* journal, for instance, excludes frequent flyer programme coordination unless it is part of a broader alliance agreement. Thirdly, the coverage of individual surveys might again vary.[27] With these caveats in mind, let us look at some of the estimates. According to *The Economist* magazine, there were 401 alliances in 1995, which was double the number it estimated four years earlier. In contrast, for 1995 and 1994, *Airline Business* estimated a total of 324 and 280 alliances respectively.[28] *Airline Business* estimated that 500 alliances among 120 participants were in force as of June 2004, while the *ICAO Journal* estimated that 600 commercial agreements among airlines were in force at the end of 2003.

Most of the studies on this topic did, however, arrive at similar conclusions, especially regarding the following trends: that the number of alliances has been growing with a significant acceleration observed in the early 1990s; that an increasingly larger proportion of alliances are informal (non-equity) rather than formal (equity); and that a large proportion of alliances are international rather than domestic (see Figure 1–7).

The broad motivations behind alliances can be identified as follows:[29]

- To get around bilateral restrictions relating to expansion in international markets
- To get around restrictions relating to mergers and acquisitions (especially relevant to equity alliances)
- To enhance the value of networks by increasing the number of destinations and the flight frequency
- To improve the quality of connections

Figure 1–7
Incidence of alliances with differing geographic scope

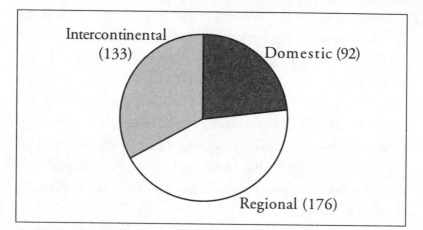

Source: Figures from the Boston Consulting Group, cited in Button et al. (1998).

- To reduce costs through economies of scale, sharing and specialization
- To gain additional market and pricing power

Alliances can take several different forms. Purchasing equity stakes (short of the levels required for a full acquisition) in another airline is a common alliance strategy that was especially popular in the 1980s and early 1990s. Equity alliances have proved to be especially attractive for international partnerships since full mergers, especially by foreign airlines, are forbidden by many host governments. In a survey by *Airline Business* in 1994, 58% of existing alliances involved the purchase of equity. This proportion, however, had dropped to 54% by 1997.

Equity alliances themselves serve a variety of purposes. They may be used to shore up a struggling partner, as in the case of KLM's cash infusion into Northwest Airlines in 1989. Sometimes, equity alliances might help the partner fend off hostile acquirers. For instance, in 1989 Delta Air Lines sold a 5% stake each to SIA and Swissair to discourage potential acquirers. If equity alliances involve mutual purchases (swaps), they serve to cement the relationship and can be an important signal that the partners value each other.

While equity alliances have positive aspects – they ensure commitment and often earn a tangible return on the investment in the form of dividends – there are downsides too. The level of control afforded by equity alliances is often less than the percentage of share ownership. The equity stake could also lose value and in some extreme cases (e.g., due to failure of the partner) become completely worthless (as in the case of SAS's stake in Continental or British Airways' stake in US Airways).[30]

A second form of arrangement is that of marketing alliances, which typically involve coordination of schedules and sharing of codes for international flights. They can have a narrow (e.g., single route) or broad scope (e.g., network-wide). Code sharing, which means that one single flight bears the codes for two or more airlines, can give the appearance of a seamless single-carrier flight to the customer. British Airways was able to extend its reach into dozens of US cities by code sharing with US Airways. According to a United Airlines manager, "The profits on offer through route-sharing are something most airlines could never hope to achieve by themselves."[31]

CHAPTER 1
◆ ◆ ◆

Block-space agreements, another type of marketing alliance, involve one airline committing itself to buying a certain number of seats on its partner's flights. If the volume of demand for the airline buying the seats is insufficient for it to operate a flight, a block-space agreement is likely to lead to cost savings. The airline that sells the seats also benefits from the higher load factor. This arrangement is useful, especially for airlines that do not have the freedoms to ply particular routes, as in Delta's block-space agreements for Virgin flights between 6–7 European cities and the United States.

Coordination of frequent flyer programmes, which offers an airline's customers the additional benefit of earning points on a partner's flights, represents a third kind of airline alliance. A typical airline might have several such agreements. Increasingly, airlines are also providing additional convenience by allowing customers to redeem miles on their partners' flights.

A recent trend in the industry is the formation of mega-alliances, such as the Star Alliance, involving sometimes a dozen or more airlines (see Figure 1–8). These alliances provide unprecedented global connectivity in addition to most of the benefits available to smaller alliances (e.g., economies of scale, customer conveniences such as access to lounges). Mega-alliances may also be in a better position to clinch corporate accounts.

Several alliances have produced substantial positive results for the partners. According to the then KLM chairman Peter Bouw, Northwest Airlines and KLM each reaped a US$220 million profit from their alliance in 1994/95, up from US$94 million in the prior year. He called the alliance "the envy of the industry" and credited it with boosting the partners' share of

Figure 1–8
Mega-alliances in the airline industry and their market shares

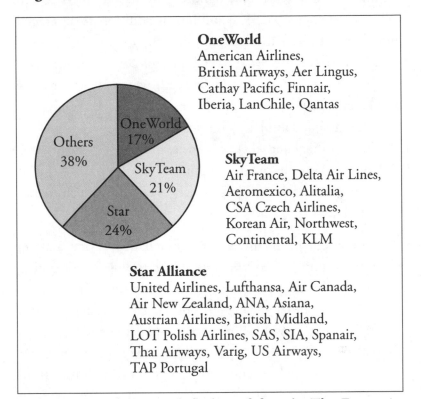

OneWorld
American Airlines,
British Airways, Aer Lingus,
Cathay Pacific, Finnair,
Iberia, LanChile, Qantas

SkyTeam
Air France, Delta Air Lines,
Aeromexico, Alitalia,
CSA Czech Airlines,
Korean Air, Northwest,
Continental, KLM

Star Alliance
United Airlines, Lufthansa, Air Canada,
Air New Zealand, ANA, Asiana,
Austrian Airlines, British Midland,
LOT Polish Airlines, SAS, SIA, Spanair,
Thai Airways, Varig, US Airways,
TAP Portugal

Source: 'Open skies and flights of fancy', *The Economist*, 2 October 2003.

North Atlantic traffic from 7% to 12% in the previous five years.[32] For OneWorld, its members expanded bilateral code shares, enhanced their computer systems to improve customer service and expected US$1 billion in benefits in 2002 "through revenue generation, protection and feed, and savings from joint purchasing and shared airport and city facilities". Meanwhile, for Star Alliance, consolidation of airport lounges and streamlined airport ground handling by its members led to collective savings of US$70 million in addition to leveraged purchasing power with other suppliers.[33]

Members of the Qualiflyer alliance, consisting of SAS, Austrian Airlines, Finnair and Swissair, were able to increase their bargaining power with aircraft manufacturers by combining their purchasing volume.

On the other hand, there is scepticism regarding the benefits of alliances in various quarters, including industry analysts who believe that the proliferation of alliances could be attributed to herd behaviour:

> Perhaps one of the drivers towards alliances is that making deals is simply good fun. Talking strategy is more exciting than examining the finer aspects of running an airline. Beating the other alliances to a deal is a buzz. There is also a feeling that, unless airlines act now, all the good partners will be lost. Like shoppers in January sales, airlines are looking for any bargains going, and not caring if they fit or not.[34]

> They're doing those things for many of the same reasons that kids join real gangs. The big airlines are seeking security and support so they can survive in one of the meanest 'hoods in the business world: the global airline industry, which is so tough that it still has a cumulative net loss for its entire history after three straight years of record profits. And the airlines are joining their high-flying, international gangs – which they call 'alliances' – because, well, everybody else is doing it.[35]

Employee scepticism of alliances is rooted in the fear about loss of jobs or cuts in pay or benefits. Members of the SkyTeam Pilots Alliance feared that high-cost SkyTeam member airlines would transfer some of their activities to operators such as Korean Air that had a substantially lower cost structure and more favourable labour pacts.[36] That may place the jobs and/or the pay of employees based in developed countries at risk.

Many alliances suffer from instability, since some partners view the arrangement as transitory while waiting for a better alternative. For instance, SAS and SIA, which used to be members of the Qualiflyer alliance and the Global Excellence Alliance, respectively, had abandoned those alliances to join the Star Alliance. The challenge in sustaining partnerships is so great that in 2003 the 14-year-old alliance between Northwest and KLM was the longest-running transatlantic airline alliance.[37] The instability rate varies across the different types of alliances' with non-equity alliances exhibiting a higher likelihood of termination (see Figure 1–9).

The key problems in alliance management include the lack of preparation before forging the alliance, over-optimistic projections about potential benefits, incompatibility of partners and/or poor management of relationships, high cost of negotiating even minor decisions, and varying commitment and service levels among the partners.

Regarding the lack of adequate preparation, one observer noted, "Alliances are a bit like marriage companies often get together thinking that they've got a lot in common and then, for the least likely reasons, things start to go wrong."[38]

Figure 1–9
Alliance types and instability rates

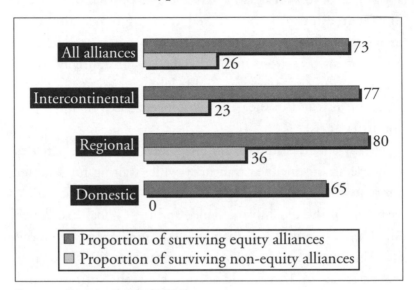

Source: Button et al. (1998).

Swissair's chief executive officer (CEO), Philip Bruggiser, whose firm was involved in many alliances, voiced the frustration of decision making in alliances: "People say they're [alliances are] a waste of time. They spend half a day talking about peanuts. We're all [alliance partners] fighting the same thing. It's the price you pay for a non-merger. When you're not independent, you're constantly negotiating."[39]

Variation in service across alliance members is another area of concern, especially for code-sharing alliances. In the block-space agreement between Delta and Virgin, some Delta customers did not like the Virgin service concept while travelling on code-shared flights operated by Virgin. One industry analyst noted, "Alliances are not the glue to create a seamless service product."[40]

Budget carriers

The airline industry has witnessed additional turbulence with the entry of airlines adopting new business models referred to as low-cost carriers, no-frills airlines or budget carriers. While budget carriers, such as Southwest Airlines, have been competing in the US market for more than 30 years, they have proliferated in Europe only over the last 10 years and are at an early stage of development in Asia Pacific and the rest of the world. Prominent examples of budget airlines include Ryanair and EasyJet (Europe), VirginBlue (Australia), WestJet (Canada), Air Do and Skymark (Japan), AirAsia (Malaysia), and ValuAir, JetStar and Tiger Airways (Singapore). The proliferation of budget carriers has been so rapid that four out of every five airline markets (i.e., the areas served by a pair of airports) now feature a budget carrier.[41] The business model of budget carriers encompasses the following characteristics:

- Single country or narrow regional (e.g., Europe, Southeast Asia) coverage, thus eliminating the need to pay overseas allowances to crew.
- A standardized fleet consisting of one type of aircraft (or variants of a family such as Boeing 737), which reduces maintenance and repair costs and ensures that pilots can hop across routes.
- Higher utilization of aircraft. It was estimated that British Midland, a conventional airline, used a plane for 8.4

hours a day, while EasyJet pushed up the utilization rate to 10.7 hours. Southwest Airlines' average utilization rate for a Bocing 737 was 11.3 hours per day versus only 9.8 hours for Delta.[42] The higher utilization is made possible by using less congested secondary airports to achieve faster turnaround time that can be as low as 20 minutes, operating point-to-point rather than hub-and-spoke service, and not assigning seat numbers to facilitate embarkation.

- Booking (for most budget carriers) through the Internet to save on travel agents' commissions, which could be as high as 9%; the cost of handling paper tickets; and wages paid to reservation agents, as budget carriers have fewer of these agents and they are typically paid minimum wages.

- Higher seating density typically in a single class configuration.

- Continuously seeking ways to reduce costs. Almost all budget carriers have minimal cabin service (e.g., no free meals), which reduces the number of flight attendants needed. Other measures include making aircraft seats non-reclinable since reclining seats are prone to breakdown, eliminating window blinds on new planes (saving US$240,000 per plane) and doing away with back-of-seat pockets as they are difficult to clean.[43]

- Usage of secondary airports, which typically have much lower landing, parking and other charges, in cities with minimum catchment areas. Interestingly, budget carriers in Japan have been constrained owing to the absence of this factor (e.g., landing slots at Tokyo's Narita Airport).[44]

Table 1–4 compares the business model of a conventional airline with that of a budget carrier. The substantially different business model of budget carriers leads to tremendous cost

Table 1–4
A conventional versus a budget carrier

	Lufthansa	EasyJet
Staff	93,246	3,453
Turnover	15,900 million euros	557 million euros
Profit	1,654 million euros (down 40%)	63 million euros (up 69%)
Load factor	73.1%	84%
Passengers	45.4 million (up 3.4%)	20.3 million (up 78%)
Fleet	382 planes, 16 different types	84 planes, 2 different types
Destinations	347 destinations in 92 countries worldwide	44 destinations in 13 countries in Europe
Departments	Logistics, maintenance, catering, travel, information technology, passenger, and other activities	Call centre, airport operations, cabin crew, and management

Sources: Lufthansa's and EasyJet's annual reports (2003).

savings (see Figure 1–10), enabling them to undercut the fares of conventional rivals. Take for example a trip from London to Glasgow, EasyJet and Go in December 2001 offered fares that were 40% lower than British Airways, 50% lower than British Midland and even lower than the train fare, although the train journey took four times as long.[45] Ryanair discounted its London to Dublin fares to as low as £9 (about US$13), compared to the £209 charged by conventional airlines at the time of its entry, and London to Venice (or Glasgow) to £8 roundtrip.[46]

While gaining increasing acceptance among price-sensitive customers, many budget carriers have found survival to be difficult. Some of the early, and storied, budget carriers such as People Express and Laker Airways did not survive for long. Even among the recent start-ups, several such as Debonair (UK) and Color Air (Norway) folded up within the first few years, while others (e.g., Go) have been absorbed by other budget carriers after suffering continual losses.

Industry observers are wondering whether many budget carriers would survive in the long run, especially if their cost advantage is diluted over time for various reasons. First, airports that have granted the budget carriers favourable terms initially may not continue to do so at the time of contract renewal, especially if there are multiple budget carriers serving the same secondary airport. Secondly, as their employees gain seniority, budget carriers' staff costs might inch up. For profitable budget carriers, their employees might demand a share of the profits. Thirdly, as new entrants flood the market (including budget carriers started by conventional airlines), price competition will

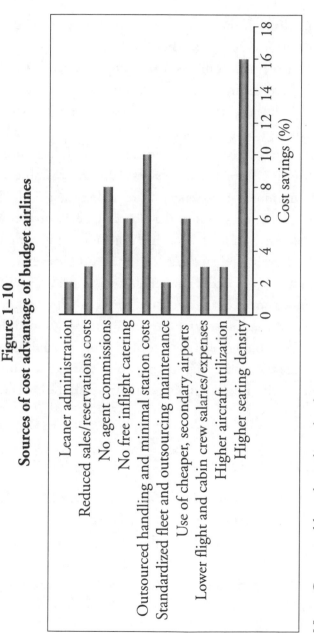

Figure 1–10
Sources of cost advantage of budget airlines

Note: Computed based on short-haul routes.
Source: Doganis (2001), p. 150.

certainly intensify. If the capacity utilization drops (e.g., due to excess capacity), it might further erode the cost advantages enjoyed by these firms. Fourthly, many budget carriers have fallen prey to the herd instinct. Lured by steep discounts offered by Boeing and Airbus during the trough of the airline business cycle, budget carriers such as Ryanair and EasyJet have ordered a large number of aircraft. According to one estimate, to fully utilize the aircraft on order, Ryanair and EasyJet will have to more than double the number of passengers carried between mid-2004 and 2008 – a tall order given the flood of new entrants and the uncertain environment (e.g., high oil prices and potential terrorism).[47] Finally, budget carriers are increasingly overlapping with the competitive space of charter airlines, which sell packages to holiday tour operators and account for as much as a third of the leisure traffic in Europe. Charter airlines have a similar lean cost structure as budget carriers yet offer more flexibility (e.g., they allow cancellation of flights that do not have a minimum load factor), which might put further pressure on the load factor of budget airlines.

Strategic Imperatives

To flourish in an extremely difficult environment, airlines need clearly articulated and efficiently executed strategies. While there are many variants of the strategies that might lead to good performance, here we will identify the key dimensions underlying the successful strategies in the industry (see Figure 1–11).

Figure 1–11
Key success factors in the airline industry

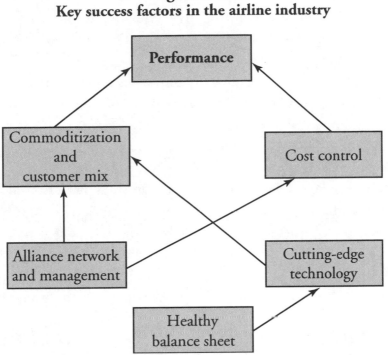

Cutting-edge technology

Deployment of cutting-edge technology remains one of the
key imperatives for airlines – especially since new technology
offers the potential to improve productivity and reduce costs,
thus mitigating the negative impact of falling yields (prices).
Successive generations of aircraft, such as the Airbus A380 to
be introduced in 2006, have dramatically raised the number
of seats and the flying range (e.g., A380 offers 35% more seats
than the Boeing 747-400). The latest aircraft also help airlines

overcome infrastructural constraints, such as the overloaded air traffic control system (e.g., by eliminating stopovers) and airport congestion, and offer better inflight facilities (e.g., bars, saunas and gymnasium in the A380).

Although often leading to improved productivity, the purchase of new planes implies significantly higher capital expenditures, with the price of a single large aircraft easily exceeding US$200 million. When these expenditures are financed with debt, they increase the risk levels given the cyclical nature of the industry and the numerous uncontrollable factors affecting its fortunes. Having a strong balance sheet is a key prerequisite to adopting cutting-edge technology, since it reduces the need for taking on debt in a cyclical industry. Even for airlines that lease, rather than buy planes, a strong balance sheet is useful for tiding over the troughs of the business cycle.

The adoption of technology goes well beyond acquiring new planes. Deployment of e-business technology can reduce maintenance costs by improving the information available to technicians maintaining the fleet and lowering material costs (e.g., through better inventory control). Air Canada Technical Service, for instance, achieved a 22% reduction in turnaround time and a 28% increase in labour productivity by using the Sinex Enterprise Resource Planning Software.[48] Distribution of tickets through the Internet can save airlines travel agent commissions and lead to better yield management. In some parts of the world where the indirect distribution channel is still prevalent, this new channel can lead to substantial improvement in revenues. According to one estimate, online sales can reduce distribution costs, which used to amount to 15%–25% of total costs in the pre-Internet days, by as much as 50%.[49]

Furthermore, technology available in the near future, such as radio frequency identification luggage tags and biometric scanning, will improve the efficiency and accuracy of several aspects of airline operations, such as check-in, boarding and baggage tracking. Technology deployment can also increase the choice of customer conveniences, which may in turn build up customer loyalty, improve load factors and enhance the revenue potential. The most obvious application in this area is inflight entertain-ment such as video on-demand.

Cost control

Given the difficult economics of the airline industry, cost control is one of the strategic priorities for airlines. As noted at the beginning of the chapter, however, many elements of airline costs (e.g., fuel, airport charges) are 'uncontrollable'. Hence, airlines have often focused on labour cost savings to improve results, especially in lean times, as quoted by Mr Weber, CEO of Lufthansa: "If we do not want to make losses again, we have to do something about our personnel costs. Otherwise I can calculate right now when we go bust, at what ticket price."[50]

Many airline managers, however, erroneously assume that wage levels are the sole determinant of labour costs while forgetting that productivity is the other important element of the equation. Poor productivity can translate even low wages into high labour costs. Many state-owned airlines from developing countries, despite having low wage costs, have high labour costs (as a proportion of total costs) because of overstaffing, which itself may be attributed to unions and government intervention.[51] Within the developed country context, adversarial labour–management relations have undermined the competitive position of the once-dominant American Airlines. According to an American judge, "If you would look up bad labor relations in the dictionary, you would have an American Airlines logo beside it."[52] The company also serves as an effective illustration of the disastrous consequences of poor labour–management relations. In May 1994, conflicts between the unions and CEO Robert Crandall forced American Airlines to stop selling tickets on 20% of its flights and cancel another 40% of the flights. Losses came to US$10 million per day for five days. The then US president Bill Clinton had to intervene to resolve the issue.[53]

On the other hand, high productivity can lead to significant benefits for the company. An analysis of European airlines shows that there are large variations in productivity across airlines based in the same country (e.g., British Caledonian versus British Airways) and that productivity and the overall performance of the airline are positively correlated.[54] In the United States, Southwest Airlines, famous for its employee-centred corporate culture, outperforms its rivals in terms of a variety of productivity metrics:

- Southwest needs only 80 workers to fly and support each aircraft, compared with 115 or more at a conventional network carrier.

- For operating an identical aircraft model (Boeing 737-300) Southwest's direct operating costs per seat-mile are 36%–44% lower than network carriers such as Delta Air lines and United Airlines. This differential exists despite a longer stage length (of 40% or more) for Delta and United.[55]
- The average number of hours flown by a Southwest pilot is 62 versus 36 for United.
- The output per employee is 20% higher at Southwest than at United, though Southwest operates smaller-capacity aircraft and flies shorter distances.[56]

Striving to improve productivity, rather than controlling wage costs, also makes sense because wage levels are significantly influenced by the context in which the airline is operating, including local laws (e.g., governing employee benefits or unions), the level of unionization and the cost of living, and hence are less controllable.

Managing alliances

Alliances generate mixed reactions from industry executives partly because of their different degrees of success. While alliances may not have been the top strategic choice for many airlines, they do serve useful purposes as suggested by the positive results achieved by the Northwest–KLM, OneWorld and Star alliances. Alliances may also be inescapable since an increasingly larger proportion of customers require global connectivity. In a world where lean cost structures may be essential to survival, airlines can also ill afford to keep performing activities where they lack economies of scale, or do not have the best-in-class skills, and must cede these activities to their alliance partners.

Alliances may be particularly useful in lean times when schedule coordination, reciprocal service provision (e.g., maintenance, check-in) and economies of scale through pooled purchasing are vital. Alexander Rahe, Star Alliance's director of sales for North Americas, said, "[After 11 September] we are really seeing the synergies and revitalization within the alliance."[57]

Alliances are also valuable in the sense that they have fewer hidden costs than mergers and hence would be important even in a world where there are no regulatory barriers. Mergers lead to fleet diversity, which raises a variety of costs, such as maintenance and repair costs, crew salaries and other labour costs. If mergers are financed through debt, they increase risk. Even if further dismantling of regulatory barriers makes mergers and acquisitions possible, we believe that alliances will remain an important strategic option for airlines, contrary to the belief of some industry analysts and managers.

We do not intend to argue that alliances are easy to manage or that all alliances lead to positive results. Given the potential benefits of alliances, however, we believe that alliances are worth considering. Airline managers should strive to make their alliances successful rather than de-emphasizing or abandoning them. They might also do well to take alliance instability as a given (after all, low entry and exit costs are two key benefits of alliances) and work towards developing their 'alliance competence'. Alliances that have obtained the best results have typically brought together partners with complementary capabilities (as in the case of the Northwest–KLM alliance) and compatible cultures as well as service levels. Members of successful alliances have also worked assiduously towards making the alliances work by focusing on the synergies and positive results rather than the differences.

Avoiding the herd instinct

The cyclical nature of the airline industry makes airline executives vulnerable to making decisions – seemingly appropriate at least in the short run – regarding aircraft acquisition and staff wages that might come back to haunt them later. In the second half of the 1980s, based on optimistic projections of traffic growth, airline executives went on an aircraft acquisition spree which led to 7,000 aircraft being placed on order for delivery between 1990 and 2001 representing a financial commitment of US$400 billion.[58] When the traffic growth did not materialize because of recession and the Gulf war, many planes were put up for sale.[59] Interestingly, many of these planes were acquired at bargain prices by new entrants – the budget carriers – which would later compete vigorously with the traditional carriers. The excess capacity in the industry also led to some destructive fare wars, as occurred in the United States in 1992.

Several industry executives have expressed their concern about the decision-making process in airlines:

I think, historically, the airline business has not been run as a real business. That is, a business designed to achieve a return on capital that is then passed on to shareholders. It has historically been run as an extremely elaborate version of a model railroad, that is, one in which you try to make enough money to buy more equipment (Michael Levine, executive vice president of Northwest Airlines, taken from www.skygod.com/quotes/airlines.html).

None of them [the traditional airlines] seem to have the idea that perhaps they had *too* many aeroplanes, perhaps they were spending too much money on aeroplanes and not enough getting the aeroplanes in the air for the right number of hours[60] (Sir Freddie Laker, founder of the now-defunct Laker Airways).

As noted earlier, aircraft acquisition decisions need to be based on an exceptionally long time horizon. They cannot simply be based on the current state of the economy (or on projections that assume the economy will continue to develop into the future) and the industry. The decisions must also make economic sense not only under rosy scenarios but also in a less favourable political and economic environment.

Commoditization and customer mix

To overcome the commoditization of its service and gain customer loyalty, American Airlines launched the first frequent flyer (FF) programme in 1981, and other airlines soon followed suit. Many airlines, however, were too generous in granting FF points and in the process built up massive contingent liabilities (in the form of FF points that may be exchanged for free travel). To contain the problem, they implemented complex restrictions on their FF programme, alienating customers in the process. It may be an opportune time for airlines to reexamine their FF programmes and adopt a sensible strategy where they reward customer loyalty in a fashion that does not undermine profitability or alienate customers. Interestingly, a recent survey found that FF programmes were the least important driver of customer satisfaction, behind factors such as airport check-in, flight availability and scheduling, and flight attendants.[61] The FF policies of many successful carriers are noteworthy. SIA and Qantas do not award FF points for deeply discounted fares and thus eliminate one of the key sources of inequity in most FF programmes, and that is same mileage credit without regard to the fare paid. Southwest Airlines has made its FF programme valuable by placing no limits on available seats to FF members; if a seat is available on a particular flight, it can be obtained in exchange for FF points.

Airlines also need to reflect on whether they have done too much discounting while trying to neutralize the perishable nature of the service. According to one estimate, 54% of all fares purchased by US domestic travellers are more than 50% below the industry's average fare. If the customers of budget airlines are included, 78% of the seats are sold at steep discounts, accounting for only 26% of the revenues. As noted by the editor of an industry magazine, "The freedom to cut prices is a valuable competitive tool in private businesses, but the airline use of this tool in the early years of deregulation has turned into a compulsion."[62]

Budget carriers have introduced innovative strategies to entice price-sensitive customers by unbundling the various components of airline service. Ryanair's ticket price, for instance, does not include the conveniences taken for granted by conventional airline passengers, such as check-in bags. The money made from these extra services could be an important source of revenues. The airline also hopes to increase its revenues through services such as live pay-per-view television, hotel bookings, car hire, online shopping and Internet gambling.

In comparison, the 13% of the network airlines' passengers who pay high fares, produce 38% of the revenues.[63] One survey suggests that many airlines are doing a poor job of satisfying even these high-paying customers, with only 45% of business customers being satisfied. Interestingly, conventional airlines with an extensive network, such as Lufthansa and British Airways, are potentially in an excellent position to serve these passengers, since they offer superior connectivity and higher levels of service, but they seem to be missing the opportunity.

In Conclusion

Adopting the whole airline industry as the unit of analysis, this chapter reviewed its historical development, important trends over time and key aspects of the industry economics. One of the key conclusions drawn from this review is that the industry poses tremendous challenges to the incumbents, especially with regard to attaining consistent profitability. We also identified a few strategies that could help the incumbents mitigate the difficulties existing in the operating environment. These strategies include the adoption of cutting-edge technology, effective cost control and labour management, managing alliances for synergies, avoiding the herd instinct in adopting technology or purchasing new equipment, as well as avoiding commoditization of services and focusing on the appropriate customer mix.

NOTES

1   *ICAO Journal,* September 2004.
2   *The National Impact of Civil Aviation,* a report by DRI WEFA Inc. and the Campbell-Hill Aviation Group, July 2002, cited in Taneja (2002).
3   *ICAO Journal,* no. 6 (2004).
4   Revenue passenger-kilometre is the number of revenue passengers on each flight multiplied by the distance flown.
5   Taneja (2002), p. 185; Doganis (1991); Oum (1997).
6   Taneja (2002).
7   Residents of cities such as Singapore and Hong Kong undertake the highest number of trips on a per capita basis.
8   Taneja (2002); 'Minister seeks to right S'pore–Aussie air links imbalance', *Straits Times* (Singapore), 8 February 2005, p. 3.
9   'Virtual mergers: With traditional mergers difficult to pull off, airlines are finding creative way to consolidate', *Investment Dealer's Digest: IDD,* 31 January 2000, p. 1.
10 Doganis (2001); Taneja (2003).
11 *ICAO Journal,* no. 6 (2003); Taneja (2003).
12 While some of the exchange risk can be hedged, hedging is neither costless nor does it eliminate the risk completely.
13 Taneja (2002); 'High fuel prices spark Southwest buyouts, UAL loss', 28 May 2004, www.smartmoney.com.
14 'Awful days ahead: Ryanair CEO', *Business Times* (Singapore), 15 September 2004.
15 Taneja (2003).
16 Ott and Neidl (1995).
17 Taneja (2003).
18 Taneja (2003).

[19] While there is a ready secondary market for used aircraft, the prices for used aircraft vary significantly and tend to be quite low during the industry's recessionary periods.

[20] Doganis (1991).

[21] Taneja (2003).

[22] Taneja (2002); Ott and Neidl (1995).

[23] An industry executive quoted in Ott and Neidl (1995).

[24] Cited in Holloway (2003), p. 581.

[25] Taneja (2002), p. 15.

[26] *www.planecrashinfo.com/cause.htm*. Risks based on data between 1987 and 1996.

[27] The *Airline Business* survey, for instance, focuses on the top 200 airlines.

[28] Ott and Neidl (1995).

[29] Taneja (2003).

[30] Glisson et al. (1996).

[31] Cyril Murphy, vice president for international affairs at United Airlines, quoted in *Airfinance Journal*, 11 October 1997, p. 36.

[32] 'KLM chief puts alliance benefits at $220 million for each partner', *Airline Financial News*, 3 July 1995, p. 1

[33] 'Star alliance membership still shines the brightest', *Business Travel News*, 8 April 2002.

[34] 'Marry in haste, repent at leisure', *Airfinance Journal*, no. 229 (June 2000): 7.

[35] 'Alliances changing the airlines industry', *Journal Record*, 12 November 1998, p. 1.

[36] 'Global unionization: SkyTeam member airlines' pilot unions tighten cooperative links as the alliance prepares to expand', *Aviation Week and Space Technology*, 22 September 2003, p. 44.

[37] 'Northwest alliance with KLM Royal Dutch Airlines at risk', *Memphis Business Journal*, 8 August 2003, p. 12.

[38] Fariba Allandari of Cranfield University quoted in *Airfinance Journal*, 11 October 1997, p. 36.

[39] 'Swissair: Time to deliver', *Air Transport World*, 1 June 1997, p. 30.

[40] See note 9.

[41] *The Economist*, 27 March 2004.

[42] Doganis (2001), p. 131.

[43] 'Ryanair taking no-frills flying to new heights: Report', *USA Today*, 16 February 2004, *www.usatoday.com*.

[44] Taneja (2003).

[45] Taneja (2002).

[46] 'Airline zen: Less is more', *www.thetravelinsider.info.*

[47] 'Turbulent skies: Low cost airlines', *The Economist,* 10 July 2004, p. 68.

[48] 'Airlines are adopting complex software solutions to streamline their maintenance departments', *Air Transport World,* January 2004, p. 54.

[49] Taneja (2003).

[50] Jurgen Weber, CEO of Lufthansa, quoted by *The Times,* 27 February 1997, cited in Doganis (2001).

[51] Job preservation may be a condition imposed by the government for shoring up the airline.

[52] US district judge Joe Kendall issuing a restraining order against an American Airlines pilots' union sickout, 10 February 1999.

[53] Ott and Neidl (1995), p. 37.

[54] Button et al. (1998).

[55] Doganis (2001), p. 131. Economics suggests that the airline with the longer stage length should have lower costs.

[56] Taneja (2003).

[57] See note 33.

[58] Doganis (1991).

[59] The number of aircraft available for sale or lease peaked at 854 in mid-1991 and remained at approximately 700 through 1993 (Ott and Neidl, 1995, p. 17).

[60] 'That was then and this is now: Sir Freddie Laker', *http://news.bbc.co.uk/ 1/hi/uk/2283244.stm.*

[61] Taneja (2002).

[62] William H. Gregory, former editor-in-chief of *Aviation Week and Space Technology,* quoted in Ott and Neidl (1995).

[63] Taneja (2003).

REFERENCES

Button, Kenneth, Kingsley Haynes and Roger Stough (1998). *Flying into the Future.* Cheltenham: Edward Elgar.

Doganis, Rigas (1991). *Flying Off Course: The Economics of International Airlines* (2nd ed.). New York: Routledge.

———. *The Airline Business in the Twenty-First Century.* London: Routledge.

Glisson, L.M., Cunningham, W.A., Harris, J.R., and Di Lorenzo-Aiss, J., 'Airline industry strategic alliances: Marketing and policy implications', *International Journal of Physical Distribution & Logistics Management*, Vol. 26, No. 3.

Holloway, Stephen (2003). *Straight and Level: Practical Airline Economics*. Aldershot: Ashgate.

Ott, James, and Raymond E. Neidl (1995). *Airline Odyssey: The Airline Industry's Turbulent Flight into the Future*. New York: McGraw-Hill.

Oum, Tae Hoon (1997). 'Challenges and opportunities for Asian airlines and governments'. In Christopher Findlay, Chia Lin Sien and Karmjit Singh (eds), *Asia Pacific Air Transport*. Singapore: Institute of Southeast Asian Studies.

Taneja, Nawal K. (2002). *Driving Airline Business Strategies through Emerging Technology*. Aldershot: Ashgate.

———. (2003). *Airline Survival Kit: Breaking out of the Zero Profit Game*. Aldershot: Ashgate.

2

Key Drivers of Singapore Airlines' Performance: Strategic Choices and Resource Deployment Decisions

This chapter focuses on the contribution of key strategic choices and resource deployment decisions to SIA's superior performance. We focus on seven broad factors which we believe to be the most salient. These are (in no particular order of importance) low staff costs, exposure to competition, a young aircraft fleet, a global revenue base, brand reputation, response to

crises, and alliance and acquisition strategies. Besides having
significant individual impacts on SIA's performance, some of
these factors also interact with one another thereby enhancing
the magnitude of their impacts (see Figure 2–1). We shall identify
how each of these factors enhances SIA's performance.

Figure 2–1
Factors accounting for SIA's superior performance

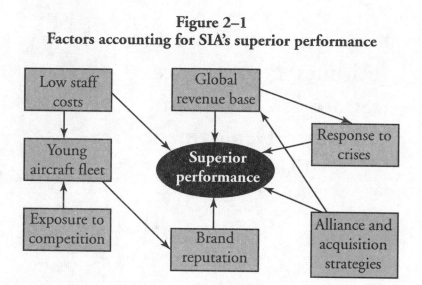

Brand Reputation

SIA is among the few airlines that have a very strong and positive
brand reputation. A recent survey placed the value of the SIA
brand at S$332 million, the seventh highest among Singaporean
companies.[1] The high brand value is a result of conscious
decisions and strategies implemented over a long period of time.
According to Dr Cheong Choong Kong, SIA's former chairman
and CEO:

The Singapore Girl was conceived, a personification of oriental charm and friendliness, which the airline made real through careful recruitment and painstaking training. Effective and original advertising, together with word of mouth praises from satisfied passengers, would create an aura of superior service and style. The aura, once established, had to be sustained through constant training, clever advertising and ingenuity in the cabin.[2]

SIA's branding strategy is notable in several other aspects. It adopts a global approach to advertising by using the same advertisement (containing the same message, except in different languages) in international media as well as in overseas markets. Moreover, the broad basis of its brand positioning (the Singapore Girl, a great way to fly, and latest fleet) has been consistently emphasized since its inception. Many other airlines, on the other hand, have changed their advertising theme every few years, thus confusing the customer.[3] To build and sustain its brand reputation, SIA's advertising investments are heavy and are maintained even during industry downturns. During the first 21 years of its existence, SIA invested as much as S$750 million in advertising (an average of S$35 million per year, but expenditures in recent years might have been significantly higher).

Interestingly, SIA's brand-building efforts witnessed tremendous success in the first few years after the launch of its advertising campaign, leading to a first mover advantage. In 1973, the year the campaign was launched, the recall rate of the advertisement was 21%; by 1979 it had jumped to 50%.[4] Being a pioneer in the industry in terms of brand building, SIA's established reputation is difficult to overcome by later adopters of even a similar strategy. SIA's success in branding was acknowledged by Madame Tussauds when the Singapore Girl became the only commercial figure in the world-famous wax museum. The museum described the Singapore Girl as "one of the world's most instantly recognizable faces".[5]

Young Aircraft Fleet

Maintaining a young fleet has been a core element of SIA's strategy since its inception. In the 1980s, it was able to maintain the fleet age at around 30 months. Since 1994, though its average fleet age has risen to between 60 and 70 months (see Figure 2–2), it remains much lower than the industry average of more than ten years.

SIA derives several visible and apparent benefits from maintaining a young fleet. New aircraft, based on the latest technology, are more fuel efficient. The lower fuel costs have enabled SIA to outperform many of its rivals on a relative basis during periods of high oil prices. Also, young aircraft typically cost less to maintain and need only scheduled maintenance which can be carried out at home base by SIA's own technicians. The reliability of a young fleet also means that SIA seldom needs to call in outside agencies to address technical problems that develop in foreign locations, which would incur high costs. With fewer breakdowns, SIA avoids the additional costs due to delayed flights or missed connections (e.g., meal vouchers, marketing inducements such as frequent flyer miles, and sometimes

Figure 2–2
Size and age of SIA's fleet

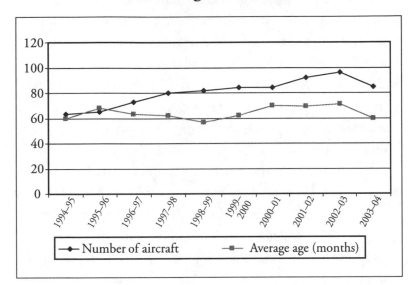

overnight hotel stays for passengers). The higher reliability of a young fleet also means better on-time performance, an important criterion for business travellers. Lastly, newer, modern aircraft bring enhanced passenger appeal.

As Figure 2–2 shows, SIA has been able to maintain the average age of the fleet even during difficult economic times such as the Asian economic crisis in 1997/98 and the industry downturn following the 11 September terrorist attacks in 2001, when profits and a positive cash flow were elusive for most airlines.

Aircraft acquisitions help SIA keep its fleet young. Even in its early days, SIA announced the largest aircraft orders in the history of the industry, including one for US$1 billion in 1978 and another two amounting to US$1.4 billion each in 1981 and 1983. Almost ten years later, in 1994 and 1995, two more large orders were announced which would determine the structure of SIA's fleet up to 2004. SIA's fleet acquisition is aimed at meeting long-term demand projections and, typically, does not fluctuate in response to short-term issues, as former CEO and chairman J. Y. Pillay explained, "Short and medium term problems cannot blind us to the needs of the future. We have to ensure that when demand resumes its growth we shall be in a position to meet it."[6]

As for the timing of aircraft acquisition, Dr Cheong explained in 1985, "A very important factor that cannot be overlooked is the timing of the order. The last big order was made in 1983, under recessionary conditions for airlines and airlines manufacturers. Orders for equipment were few and far between, and manufacturers were generous with concessions to get their production lines moving. Both Boeing and Airbus were eager to establish a foothold in Asia for their new aircraft – the B757 and the A310 respectively."[7]

Consistently high profitability and cash flow from operations are the key facilitating factors for its aircraft acquisitions, which in turn may be attributed to its low costs and differentiated products.

Low Staff Costs Yet High Productivity

Some industry observers attribute the success of Asian airlines, including SIA, to their lower wage costs compared with airlines in developed countries (see Figure 2–3). It is also often argued that the higher wage costs of many developed country airlines are

Figure 2–3
Labour costs as a percentage of total operating costs

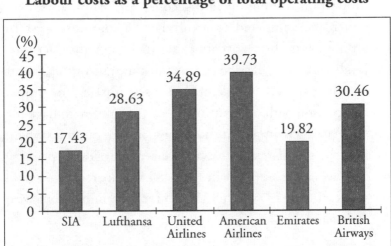

Note: The figures for SIA, Emirates and British Airways refer to the 2003–2004 financial year. Those for the other airlines are for the 2003 year. The figures for Lufthansa include its non-airline operations.

Sources: Annual reports of the respective airlines.

due to local labour laws and, hence, are outside their control. Conversely, Asian carriers (or airlines based in developing countries, in general) do not have to contend with strict labour laws (e.g., laws protecting employee benefits, such as minimum wage and health insurance, or prohibiting age discrimination) and hence enjoy a cost advantage. SIA's top management, however, has always refuted the claim that lower wages are the only determinant of its competitive advantage and superior performance, but has instead emphasized the role of the superior productivity of its employees. Former chairman Dr Cheong said in 1985:

The fact is that SIA's staff costs are not low. It is true that in proportion to total operating costs, SIA's staff costs are a low 21%, compared to around 30% for most western airlines, but this is attributable to higher productivity. [Staff costs here include the cost of the staff in the airport handling and engine maintenance subsidiaries, for proper comparison with other airlines.] ... If SIA were to have the same productivity as British Airways, its staff numbers would have to rise and its staff costs as a percentage of total operating costs would be over 26% in 1983–84. This percentage would rise further to 29% with SAS' productivity and 34.6% with Swissair's.[8]

Analysis by independent industry experts also supports SIA's position. One analysis showed that Asian carriers generally had higher output per US$1,000 of labour costs, suggesting that lower wage rates did play a role (see Figure 2–4). However, it also showed that there were significant variations in productivity among Asian carriers themselves, with SIA showing a sizeable advantage over the next best airline.

There are many drivers of productivity at SIA. First of all, its staff turnover is low. In 1996, 19% of its employees had been with the company for more than 20 years.[9] Another is the large investments in state-of-the-art equipment and training. For instance, SIA was a pioneer in the installation of flight simulators, which are valuable in the training of pilots. It is noteworthy that, despite a series of crises affecting the fortunes of the industry between 1997 and 2003 (e.g., Asian

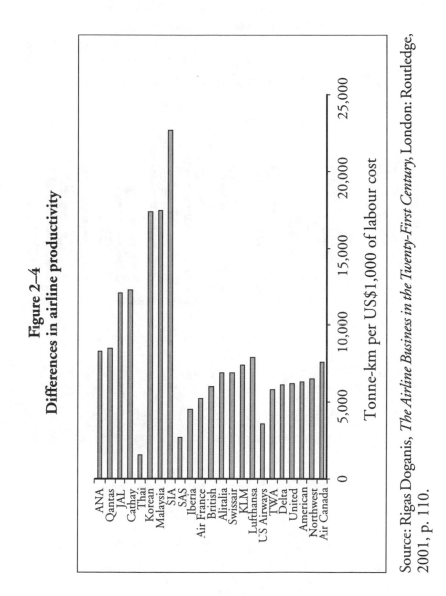

Figure 2–4
Differences in airline productivity

Tonne-km per US$1,000 of labour cost

Source: Rigas Doganis, *The Airline Business in the Twenty-First Century*, London: Routledge, 2001, p. 110.

economic crisis, 11 September attacks, SARS), SIA has been able to regain its productivity each time (see Figure 2–5).

Figure 2–5
Value added per employee for the SIA Group

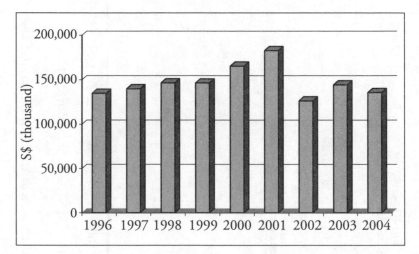

In 2000, the company started granting stock options to employees at all levels. Thanks to its consistently superior financial performance, these options are likely to be perceived as valuable by employees and hence act as a source of motivation and a driver of productivity.[10]

Exposure to Competition

In the highly regulated airline industry, where decisions about forming airlines and supporting them through regulation of flying rights as well as direct subsidies are driven more by national pride than by economic soundness, SIA remains a notable exception. While the government (through Temasek Holdings) remains the majority owner to this day, and the board of SIA is nominated by the government, there has been surprisingly little government intervention in SIA's operations. As former deputy managing director (Commercial) and vice president (Marketing) for SIA, Michael Tan pointed out in 1993:

> Right from the beginning, the Singapore government made it clear that we were to operate profitably or not at all. Singapore could not afford a national carrier for the sake of pride alone. ... Singapore's skies were opened and foreign carriers welcomed. This policy has benefited Singapore, the travellers and shippers, and established Changi as a key international and regional aviation hub, today served by 59 airlines to 109 cities. But it also meant that SIA had to compete at the outset as a commercial entity. Although the government is the majority shareholder and the Board is nominated by them, it plays no direct role in running the company.[11]

The lack of government protection turned out to be a blessing in disguise. Forced to compete with larger and well-established airlines from other parts of the world, SIA developed one of the most efficient cost structures among all airlines. Despite the low yields due to stiff competition, and the long average stage length of its flights, it was able to turn profits because its costs were even lower.[12] The substantial difference between yields and unit costs means that SIA maintains a positive cash flow in most years, which allows it to fund aircraft acquisitions, without the need for debt financing (see Figure 2–6). The

Figure 2–6
Cash-flow generation and capital expenditures by SIA

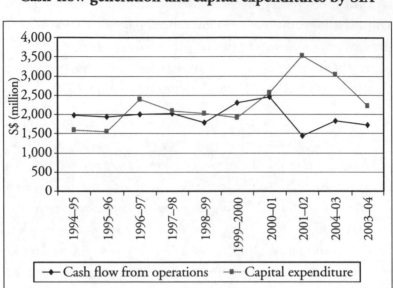

healthy cash flow also allows it to time aircraft purchases during industry downturns (to take advantage of discounts) and to fund brand-building and service-enhancement initiatives.

Global Revenue Base

Having a global presence is another key strength of SIA. The company takes pride in the fact that it is not dependent on any one geographic region for its revenues. Even when the Asian region was growing much faster than other parts of the world (from the late 1980s to 1997), it did not make the mistake of neglecting the rest of the world, and Mr Pillay asserted that "no country or route accounts for more than 15% of our revenue".[13] In 1991, the *Far Eastern Economic Review* noted that SIA earned twice as much outside Asia than did Cathay Pacific, itself a high-profile global airline.[14] Figure 2–7 shows the global distribution of SIA's revenues at three different points in time.

The benefits of a globally diversified revenue base are twofold. First, adverse economic conditions which might affect traffic patterns in a particular geographic region (e.g., the decline in traffic to and from the United States following the 11 September attacks) will have less of an impact on SIA. In fact, SIA's diversified revenue base allows it to flourish in the affected regions at the expense of geographically focused carriers (as in the case of Garuda Indonesia during the Asian economic crisis). Secondly, a global presence enables SIA to offer superior connectivity to customers.

Response to Crises

Since 1997, SIA has been through a number of crises. Interestingly, neither industry-wide crises such as the 11 September attacks nor company-specific crises such as the crash of flight SQ006 in Taiwan have forced SIA to dilute its existing strategy. In fact, it has emerged stronger after some crises.

During the depths of the Asian economic crisis, a combination of low demand and depreciating currencies put most Asian carriers in financial hardship: Cathay Pacific made the first financial loss in its history, Korean Air was worth less than 3 of its fleet of 45 Boeing 747s jumbo jets, and Garuda witnessed its load factor plummeting from 80% to 49%. SIA was able to

Figure 2–7
Global spread of SIA's revenues

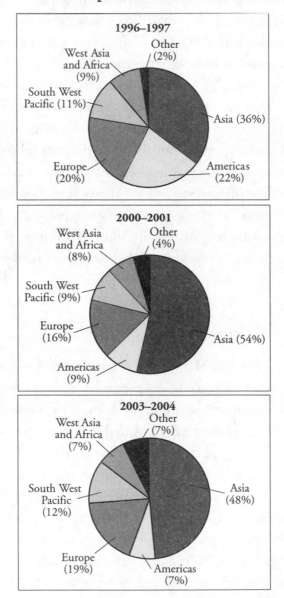

remain profitable over this period through a variety of measures, including belt-tightening measures such as capacity reduction and salary freezes coupled with promotions (some jointly with hotels) to spur demand.

In the midst of the crisis, in September 1998, SIA announced its biggest ever product launch, with brand new products and services being introduced in all three classes on its Boeing 747, Airbus A340 and Boeing 777 planes. The launch was estimated to cost S$500 million and included mini-suites complete with seat-beds and retractable desks for first class, privacy dividers and increased seat pitch, width and height for business class, improved seats enhanced with headrests and side ears for economy class, as well as improved cuisine for all classes.

In October 2000, the first major accident in SIA's history occurred when flight SQ006 crashed in inclement weather at Taiwan's Chiang Kai Shek Airport. In an effort to control the damage, SIA was quick to offer a compensation of US$400,000 to the next of kin of those killed and US$20,000 to the survivors.[15] The former figure far exceeded the sum of US$75,000 specified under the Warsaw Convention. Subsequently, SIA terminated the services of the two pilots involved in the crash, and the airline appeared to emerge unscathed.

The terrorist attacks on 11 September 2001 severely hit air travel in general and travel to and from America in particular. In the ensuing six months, SIA's earnings disappointed analysts. By January 2002, however, traffic had in fact rebounded, and within 12 months after the attacks, SIA had launched an improved business class service (including 'spacebeds' and a new inflight entertainment system) on selected routes and on almost half of its aircraft fleet. According to industry analysts, the upgrades were driven by competitive pressures in the form of similar upgrades by rivals, such as British Airways and Qantas, and the need to enhance its reputation especially in the eyes of business class customers.

In March/April 2003, airlines were buffeted by a pair of crises in the form of the US-led war in Iraq and the SARS epidemic. The eruption of SARS affected SIA in particular, since Singapore as well as some key destinations (especially Guangzhou province in China and Hong Kong, to which SIA was flying 41 times a week) had a significant number of SARS cases. SIA responded with cutbacks in capacity for the affected regions, layoffs and wage cuts. It also adopted customer-friendly policies such as allowing customers to reroute their flights without penalties or charges. As for the Iraq war, hedging contracts shielded the airline to a great extent from the rapidly escalating oil prices during the war and also in the following two years when oil prices remained high.

While the scope and impact of each crisis were different, there are several key commonalities in SIA's responses to the different crises. The first is that SIA did not shy away from making large investments aimed at improving customer conveniences even during the depths of the crises. These investments often generated positive publicity for SIA and kept it in the public eye.[16] Its accumulated strengths of healthy financial reserves and established brand reputation served it well during these difficult times. Secondly, SIA's single-minded focus on providing superior customer service helped it adopt appropriate customer-centric policies, such as allowing penalty-free rerouting for affected customers during the SARS epidemic. This focus might also explain its quick compensation offer to the victims of the SQ006 crash in Taiwan. Thirdly, SIA's top management often set the example in sharing the pain in difficult times. During the SARS crisis, top managers took the lead by cutting their own salary by 7%–15% first. Furthermore, while its labour–management relations have experienced occasional hiccups (some recent press reports suggest a significant deterioration in the relationship), it is a credit to the company that pay cuts implemented during crisis periods were restored quickly when performance improved, as it had done within a year of the 11 September attacks.

Alliance and Acquisition Strategies

Historically, a highly regulated environment prevented airlines from undertaking acquisitions and led to the formation of alliances. SIA was no exception and had formed a network of alliances by 1995 to improve access to key markets. This network included equity stakes of 5% and 2.8% in Delta Air Lines and Swissair respectively (see Figure 2–8).

Over time, SIA's alliance network grew in terms of the number of partners as well as the geographic scope. Several interesting conclusions can be drawn by examining SIA's alliance and acquisition strategies over a period of ten years between 1995 and 2004. SIA was cautious in forging alliances in its early days and operated a 'small' network of alliances in 1995. Some of its partners were low-profile airlines. By 2000, the network had grown and included a number of high-profile partners such

Figure 2–8
SIA's alliance network in various years

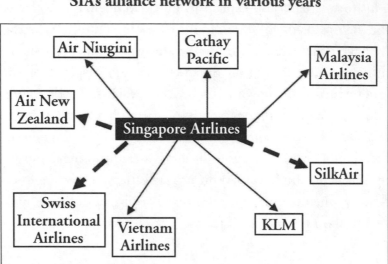

(a) 1995

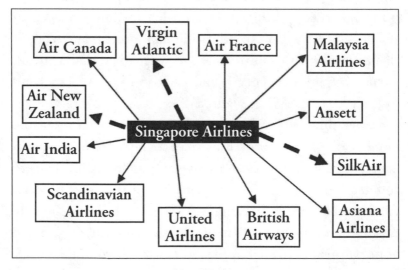

(b) 2000

Figure 2–8 (continued)

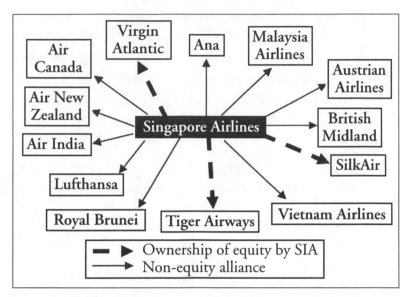

(c) 2004

Note: While SIA has joined the Star Alliance since 2000, not all the members of the alliance are shown in the figures in the interest of simplicity.

Sources: *Airline Business*, September (1996, 2001, 2004).

as United Airlines, SAS and Lufthansa. Its earlier equity relationships with Swissair and Delta had been dissolved by then and new equity relationships formed with Virgin Atlantic and Air New Zealand. The later relationships represented larger stakes which allowed SIA to participate in, and even control, the decision making of its partners. Many of SIA's alliances and acquisitions were driven by a need to extend its reach, as in its acquisition of a stake in Virgin in order to obtain flying rights to the transatlantic routes. Between 2000 and 2004, there was further turnover among SIA's alliance partners with some (e.g., Ansett) going bankrupt. Generally, SIA has been cautious in its alliance formation. Its alliance network is far less extensive than those of some of its competitors, such as Lufthansa (see Figure 2–9). SIA has been particularly conservative in forging code-sharing agreements, since its hard-earned reputation might be dented by unsatisfactory service on a partner airline's flight.

Figure 2–9
Alliance activity of SIA versus some key rivals

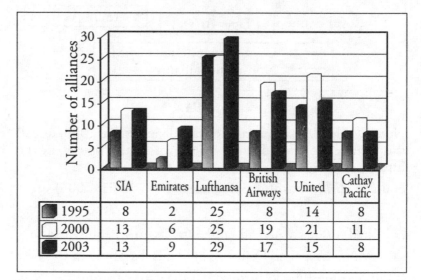

	SIA	Emirates	Lufthansa	British Airways	United	Cathay Pacific
1995	8	2	25	8	14	8
2000	13	6	25	19	21	11
2003	13	9	29	17	15	8

Sources: *Airline Business*, no. 6 (1995, 2000, 2003).

In Conclusion

This chapter examined how SIA's strategic choices and resource deployment decisions have impacted its performance. A key conclusion that can be drawn from the analysis is that SIA's superior performance is attributable to a complex array of strategic decisions which have been highly consistent over time, including maintenance of a young aircraft fleet, sustained investment in brand building, and emphasis on staff training to produce a high level of productivity. There are also inter-relations between some of the factors which add to the individual impacts of these factors. SIA's brand reputation, for instance, is linked to investment in training as well as a young aircraft fleet. The maintenance of the young fleet, in turn, is enabled by low costs (which are attributed to high employee productivity and exposure to competition) and a global presence which is supported by a cautious yet consistently pursued alliance strategy. We believe that the sustainability of SIA's competitive advantage lies in the multitude of contributing factors and the interrelationships between them, which make it difficult for imitators to match SIA's competitive advantage and superior performance by copying individual aspects of its strategy.

NOTES

1   'Loyalty beyond reason', *Business Times* (Singapore), 15 December 2004.
2   Cheong in a speech to the Young President's Organisation in Singapore on 8 February 1985, in *Perspectives* (Singapore: Communications Department, Singapore Airlines, 1998), pp. 9–17.
3   Michael Tan in a speech at the Third World Advertising Congress held in Beijing, 16–20 June 1987, in *Perspectives* (Singapore: Communications Department, Singapore Airlines, 1998), pp. 26–9.
4   International Research Associates survey results, cited in 'Singapore Airlines (A)', Harvard Business School case no. 9-687-022.
5   'Staying ahead of competition', Thoeng Tjhoen Onn speaking at the AIC Asia/Pacific Conference on Marketing Airline Services held

in Singapore on 26 August 1993, in *Perspectives* (Singapore: Communications Department, Singapore Airlines, 1998), pp. 92–6.

6   Pillay in a speech at SIA's 28th anniversary gala dinner at the Shangri-La Hotel on 17 August 1974, in *Perspectives* (Singapore: Communications Department, Singapore Airlines, 1998), pp. 7–8.

7   See note 2.

8   See note 2.

9   In *Perspectives* (Singapore: Communications Department, Singapore Airlines, 1998), p. 69.

10 The performance of SIA's stock has been inconsistent since the 1997 Asian economic crisis, with good periods alternating with challenging periods. Given its strong competitive position, however, barring poor performance of the whole sector and strategic missteps, SIA is expected to outperform the industry in the short and medium term.

11 Tan speaking to the Indonesian Business Association of Singapore on 18 March 1993, in *Perspectives* (Singapore: Communications Department, Singapore Airlines, 1998), pp. 89–91.

12 Cheong speaking at the SIA World Marketing Conference on 16 November 1995, in *Perspectives* (Singapore: Communications Department, Singapore Airlines, 1998), p. 145. Both cost and yield are dependent on stage length. SIA's average stage length is longer than most other airlines, because of its emphasis on long-haul routes. In the final analysis, what matters is that, accounting for stage length, an airline's yield should be greater than its cost.

13 Guiding principles stated by Pillay in SIA's 1990–91 annual report, p. 30.

14 'Profit formation', *Far Eastern Economic Review*, 24 June 1991.

15 'Singapore Airlines to face lawsuits over October 2000 crash', *Airline Industry Information*, 30 October 2002.

16 'Asia's class divide', *Air Transport World*, August 2002, pp. 43–4.

3

Achieving Cost-Effective Service Excellence at Singapore Airlines

SIA has attained the holy grail of strategic success: a sustainable competitive advantage. It has consistently outperformed its competitors for almost three and a half decades since its reincarnation from Malaysia–Singapore Airlines into Singapore Airlines. It has never posted a loss on an annual basis and has achieved substantial and superior returns in an industry plagued by intermittent periods of disastrous underperformance.

SIA has achieved this by managing to navigate skilfully between poles that most companies think of as distinct: delivering service excellence in a cost-effective way. SIA's list of awards for service excellence is long and distinguished. It won no less than 67 international awards and honours in 2002, 59 in 2003, and 34 in the first nine months of 2004.[1] According to Ian Batey, founder of Batey Ads, the agency that created the Singapore Girl brand and has nurtured it since the inception of the airline, "From the very first days of SIA, several things were clear in the mind of the brand owner: the airline was determined to be a highly profitable brand, and the best airline brand in the aviation industry. Quite a modest mission, would you not say, for the airline of one of the world's smallest nations!"[2]

Since Michael Porter's influential suggestion that differentiation and cost leadership are mutually exclusive strategies and that an organization must ultimately choose where its competitive advantage will lie,[3] there has been fierce debate about whether a combined cost leadership and differentiation strategy can be achieved and sustained over the longer term. SIA is living proof that the answer to both these questions is positive. It has consistently delivered premium service to some of the most demanding airline customers with sky-high expectations.

The Singapore Girl (Figure 3–1), an influential and potent brand carefully developed and safeguarded over the years, is known worldwide as the tangible embodiment of this caring, professional service. According to Batey, every SIA advertisement features the genuine article: real Singapore Girls. Batey Ads developed the icon with this image: "Physically, she has the attractive, natural looks of most young Asian women, and her trim figure is ideal

Figure 3–1
The Singapore Girl: Synonymous with SIA and personifying quality service

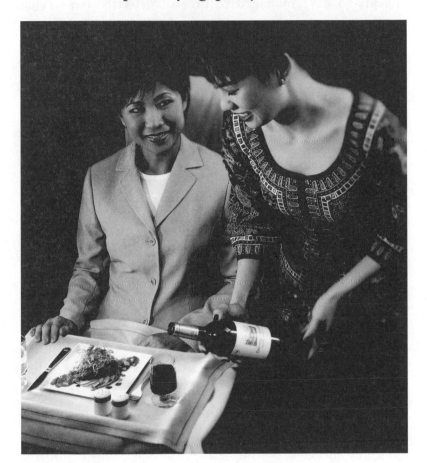

Courtesy of Singapore Airlines.

for the distinctive sarong kebaya uniform. Character-wise, she mirrors her Asian heritage – natural femininity, natural grace and warmth, and a natural, gentle way with people."[4]

| For many full-service airlines, delivering excellent service comes at a premium cost to the airline. SIA, on the other hand, appears to have managed to create cost-effective service excellence in an industry where both pricing pressures and customer expectations have been continually rising. How does it manage to do so? In common with many other organizations with a reputation for providing excellent service, SIA displays the characteristics of world-class service companies, including top management commitment, customer-focused staff and systems, and a customer-oriented culture. However, our research into SIA, spanning several years and at various levels in the organization, has uncovered a number of strategies for developing and maintaining a reputation for service excellence that will be applicable to a wide range of service organizations.

Ultimately, SIA's success is attributed to a customer-oriented culture, its recognition of the importance of its customers. According to Dr Cheong Choong Kong, SIA's former CEO, "Our passengers … are our raison d'etre. If SIA is successful, it is largely because we have never allowed ourselves to forget that important fact." However, what distinguishes SIA's customer-oriented and cost-conscious culture is that these are not just abstract, motherhood statements. The values of cost-effective service excellence are enshrined in a unique, self-reinforcing activity system that makes the values real for all employees, enacted in their every decision and action.

This activity system has five pillars, and they are (1) rigorous service design and development; (2) total innovation that integrates continuous incremental improvements with discontinuous innovations; (3) profit and cost consciousness ingrained in all employees; (4) holistic staff development; and (5) reaping of strategic synergies through related diversification and a world-class infrastructure. Figure 3–2 portrays these five elements.

Figure 3–2
The five pillars supporting SIA's cost-effective service excellence

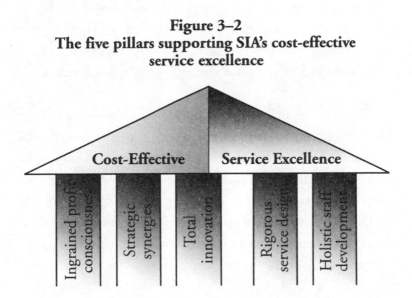

This chapter discusses these five pillars and portrays their interrelations in building an internally coherent business system that enables and safeguards the central core competency of cost-effective service excellence at SIA. The latter part of the chapter goes into some detail on SIA's strategic use of technology, specifically biometrics, to simultaneously enhance service excellence, raise efficiency as well as improve security.

Rigorous Service Design and Development

Twenty years ago, Lynn Shostack complained that service design and development was usually characterized by trial and error.[5] Unlike manufacturing organizations, where research and development departments and product engineers would routinely be found, systematic development and testing of services, or service engineering, was not the norm. Things appear to have changed little since then. For SIA, however, product design and development has always been a serious, structured issue.

SIA has a service development department, which hones and thoroughly tests any change before it is introduced. This department undertakes research, trials, time and motion studies, mock-ups, assessment of customer reaction – indeed, whatever is necessary to ensure that a service innovation is supported by the right procedures. Underpinning the continuous innovation and development processes is a corporate culture that accepts change as not just inevitable but, rather, a way of life. A trial that fails or an implemented innovation that is removed after a few months is seen as okay. In some organizations, personal reputations can be at stake and so pilot tests 'have to work'. At SIA, a failed pilot test damages no one's reputation.

In some organizations, service – and indeed product – innovations live beyond their useful years because of political pressure from management or lack of funds for continuous innovation and renewal. At SIA, it is expected that any innovation will likely have a short shelf life. The company recognizes that, to sustain its differentiation, it must maintain

continuous improvement and must kill programmes or services that no longer provide competitive differentiation: "It is
getting more and more difficult to differentiate ourselves
because every airline is doing the same thing. But the crucial
fact is that we continue to say that we want to improve, that
we have the will to do so. And every time we reach a goal, we
always say that we've got to find a new mountain or hill to
climb" (Yap Kim Wah, Senior Vice President, Product and
Service).

This emphasis on the need to continually innovate raises
the issue of sustainability of competitive advantage. SIA's
sustained superior performance relative to its peers' shows that
it has achieved this, but what is it that makes it so difficult to
imitate SIA's achievement? The secret lies in the fact that it is
easier to imitate fragments of a business system rather than the
whole system; and if such a system is internally consistent and
self-reinforcing, held together by robust, customer-focused
processes and the glue of cultural values, it becomes almost
impossible to imitate.

The stakes are raised for SIA, not only by its competitors
but also by its customers. A company with a sky-high reputation
attracts customers with sky-high expectations. SIA's research team
has found that the airline attracts a disproportionately large
number of very demanding customers who expect the best:
"Customers adjust their expectations according to the brand
image. When you fly on a good brand, like SIA, your
expectations are already sky-high. And if SIA gives anything
that is just OK, it is just not good enough" (Sim Kay Wee, Senior
Vice President, Cabin Crew).

SIA treats its customers' high expectations as a fundamental resource for innovation ideas, which it captures with its extensive customer feedback mechanisms. Weak signals are amplified, and not only written comments but even verbal comments to the cabin crew are taken seriously and reported back to the relevant sections of the airline. An additional source of intelligence is SIA's 'spy flights', whereby staff members travel on competitors' flights to gather detailed intelligence on competitive offerings.

Recognizing that its competition does not just come from within the industry, SIA sets its sights high by aiming to be not only the best airline but also the best service organization. To achieve that, it employs broad benchmarking not just against its main competitors but against the best-in-class service companies, as Mr Yap elaborates, "It is important to realize that our customers are not just comparing SIA with other airlines. They are comparing us against many industries, and on many factors. So when they pick up the phone and call up our reservations, for example, they are actually making a mental comparison, maybe subconsciously, to the last best experience they have had. It could be a hotel; it could be a car rental company. If they have had a very good experience with the hotel or car rental company and if the next call they make is to SIA, they will subconsciously make the comparison and say 'How come you're not as good as they?' They do not say 'You have the best telephone service system out of all the other airlines I've called.' Being excellent, our customers will, albeit subconsciously, benchmark us against the best in almost everything. The new ball game for SIA is not just to be the best of the best in the airline industry but to work at being the best service company."

Total Innovation Integrating Continuous Improvement with Discontinuous Innovation

An airline has a multitude of subsystems, such as reservations, catering, maintenance, inflight services and entertainment. SIA aims not to be considerably better but a little better in every one of the subsystems than its competitors. This requires not only constant innovation but also total innovation – innovation in everything, all the time. Importantly, this also supports the notion of cost-effectiveness. Continuous incremental development comes at a low cost but delivers that necessary margin of value to the customer, as Mr Yap explains, "It is the totality that counts. This also means that the innovations do not need to be too expensive. If you want to provide the best food, you might decide to serve lobster on short-haul flights between Singapore and Bangkok, for example; however, you might go bankrupt. Our strategy is to be better than our competitors in everything we do on that route, just a little bit better in everything. This allows us to make a small profit from the flight and enables us to innovate without pricing ourselves out of the market. We want to provide excellent and all-round value for money, which makes it much harder for our competitors to imitate us. Therefore, SIA comes up with new things all the time. We want to be a little bit better all the time in everything we do."

While cost-effective, incremental improvements form an important basis for its competitive advantage, SIA also implements frequent major initiatives that are firsts in its industry. One of them is its Outstanding Service on the Ground programme, which involved working with the numerous organizations providing customer service before and after a flight to ensure a seamless, efficient and caring service. SIA's latest service excellence initiative, called Transforming Customer Service, aims to build team spirit among staff in the key operational areas, which will help towards ensuring that the whole journey from making reservations onwards is as pleasant and seamless as possible for customers and staff alike. SIA employs a total innovation approach that is captured in its 40-30-30 rule to ensure a holistic approach to service improvement: 40% on training and invigorating its people, 30% on reviewing processes and procedures, and 30% on creating new product and service ideas. Total innovation means achieving cost-effective service excellence based on the totality, rather than just one aspect, of the customer experience.

In addition to continuous incremental innovations, SIA's reputation as a service innovator is also based on unanticipated, discontinuous innovations in the air. It excels at this by gaining a deep understanding of lifestyle trends and analysing their implications for the future of better service in the air. The goal of these analyses is to anticipate lifestyle changes and then to meet the new lifestyle needs. Examples of such recent innovations that help set SIA apart from its competitors include the full-size 'spacebed' and on-board e-mail and Internet services for business- and first-class passengers.

In addition, SIA has made a clear strategic choice of being a leader in innovation and a follower of innovations at the same time. While it is a pioneer of innovations related to customer service, it is at the same time a fast follower in areas that are less visible to the customer. SIA relies on proven technology that can be implemented swiftly and cost-effectively. For example, its revenue management and customer relationship management systems used proven technology in which its implementation partners had ample experience so as to ensure a smooth and cost-effective implementation, rather than going for the latest technology, which would not only be much more expensive but also carry a higher risk of implementation failure. This combination of being a leader and a follower at the same time allows SIA to maintain cost-effectiveness while innovating where it counts to the customer.

Batey describes the innovation climate at SIA as follows: "Captain Kirk of *SS Enterprise* would be in his element working at SIA, because from the day they were born they've been tireless in their mission of exploring and bringing to their customers a continuous stream of new, breakthrough service ideas. It's all part of the airline's enduring core appeal to provide a unique travel experience."[6] The two pillars of rigorous service design and development and of total innovation are amply illustrated by SIA's employment of biometric technology to offer its customers a fully automated seamless travel (FAST) experience, which will be described later.

SIA's innovation capabilities are a key part of its competitive advantage and are therefore of strategic importance. We will return to this crucial theme in Chapter 6, further expanding on the nature of strategic innovation, the reasons for which we regard SIA as a strategic innovator par excellence, and how strategic innovation can be fostered in organizations.

Profit Consciousness Ingrained in All Employees

Though totally focused on the customer and on continuous service improvement, managers and staff at SIA are well aware of the need for profitability and cost-effectiveness. The company prepares all staff from the top to the bottom to deal well with the potentially conflicting objectives of excellence and profit. This is achieved, firstly, by creating a cost and profit consciousness, according to Mr Yap: "It's drilled into us from the day we started working for SIA that if we don't make money we'll be closed down. Singapore doesn't need a national airline. Second, the company has made a very important visionary statement that 'We don't want to be the largest company. We want to be the most profitable.' That's a very powerful statement."

Any proposed innovation is analyzed very carefully on the balance between expected customer benefits and costs. Station managers and front-line staff constantly weigh passenger satisfaction against cost-effectiveness: the customer has to be satisfied, but in a cost-effective manner.

Secondly, and like many service organizations, SIA has a reward system that pays bonuses according to company performance. However, for SIA, it is the same bonus rate and formula for everyone throughout the company. As a result, there is considerable informal peer pressure within the organization, and staff appear to be quite open to challenging any decisions and actions that they deem to waste resources or involve money inappropriately spent.

Additionally, SIA builds team spirit among its 6,600 crew members by organizing them into small teams of 13 crew members who fly together as far as possible for at least two years. This leads to the development of team spirit and social bonds within the team and helps to reinforce the culture of cost-effective service excellence and the peer pressure to deliver SIA's promise to customers.

Developing Staff Holistically

Senior managers say that "training in SIA is almost next to godliness", but even this does not capture the full extent of the role of training in SIA. Everyone, no matter how senior, has a training and development plan with clear goals. New stewardesses undergo training for four months, longer than in any other airline. The training covers not only functional skills but also soft skills of personal interaction and poise as well as emotional skills for dealing with the stress arising from serving very demanding passengers. SIA's training of the Singapore Girls is likened to that in a finishing school: "The girls are transformed from coming in, and by the time they come out they look totally different. Their deportment, the way they carry themselves – there's a great transformation there," says Mr Sim.[7]

In addition to such training, SIA also encourages and supports activities that might, on the surface, appear to have nothing to do with service in the air. Cabin crew members have created groups such as the performing arts circle, which has staged full-length plays and musicals, the wine appreciation group and the gourmet circle. These activities help develop camaraderie and team spirit as well as build personal knowledge of the finer things in life, all of which raise the level of the personalized and exceptional service that the crew delivers in the air.

The staff development is continuous. As customers become more sophisticated and their expectations rise, the type of training that the Singapore Girl receives changes to cater to these demands: "While our Singapore Girl is our icon, and we're very proud of her and her achievements, we continue to improve her skills; we continue to improve her ability to understand and appreciate wines and cheeses, or our Asian heritage and so on. The enhancement must be continuous," Mr Yap stresses.

Cabin crew can select refresher courses and on average attend three to four days of such courses a year. Popular courses include transactional analysis (a counselling course), leadership, and European languages. The company is moving from a system of directing the courses cabin crew should attend to one of self-directed learning, where staff take responsibility for their own development.

Even before development starts, considerable effort is devoted to ensuring that the company hires the right staff. Entry requirements for cabin crew applicants are based on both academic qualifications (at least polytechnic diploma level, meaning that they have had 13 years of formal education) as well as physical attributes. The recruitment process is extensive, involving three rounds of interviews, a 'uniform test', a 'water confidence' test, psychometric tests, and finally a tea party to confirm the earlier assessments. Over 16,000 applications are received every year, and the company hires around 500 to 600 new cabin crew staff to cover attrition, both voluntary and directed attrition. If, for example, a stewardess becomes pregnant, she has to leave the airline. There is a scheme that allows them to apply to rejoin the airline. After the Singapore Girls start flying, they are carefully monitored for the first six months through a monthly report by the inflight supervisor. At the end of the probationary period, 75% get confirmed, around 20% get an extension of probation and 5% leave. A more detailed discussion of SIA's human resource management practices is presented in Chapter 5.

Achieving Strategic Synergies through Related Diversification and a World-Class Infrastructure

SIA utilizes related diversification in the way it was intended: to reap cost synergies and at the same time control quality and enable transfer of learning. Subsidiaries serve not only as the development ground for well-rounded management skills and a corporate rather than a divisional outlook through job rotation, but also as sources of learning.

Moreover, these related operations, such as catering, aircraft maintenance and airport management, have higher profit margins than the airline business itself because of less intense competition and more favourable industry structures. SIA Engineering Company, for example, saves the airline from having to pay expensive aircraft maintenance fees to other airlines; instead, it sells such services to other airlines at healthy margins. At the same time, being the youngest in the world, SIA's fleet incurs low maintenance costs and low fuel expenses while delivering reliable flight performance

(Figure 3–3). SIA's Inflight Catering Centre produces SIA's own inflight cuisine, ensuring high quality, reliability and responsiveness to customer feedback, and at the same time caters for other airlines at a healthy margin. SIA's SATS (Singapore Airport Terminal Services) subsidiary provides ground handling services at Changi Airport (Figure 3–4), which is regularly voted as the best airport in the world. The airport's reputation helps entice passengers travelling on to Australia, New Zealand or other countries in the region to pass through Changi and to choose SIA as their carrier.

Figure 3–3
SIA's young fleet soaring in the sky, bringing passengers
safely to their destination

Courtesy of Singapore Airlines.

SIA's subsidiaries operate under the same management philosophy and culture that emphasizes cost-effective service excellence. Even though they are part of the same group, they are quoted separately on the Singapore Exchange and are subject to market discipline with very clear profit expectations. In SIA, therefore, the conventional wisdom of outsourcing (i.e., focus

Figure 3–4
Changi Airport: World-class infrastructure and facilities that provide convenience and a wide variety of entertainment and leisure options for waiting or transit passengers

Source: *www.asiatraveltips.com/PicturesofSingaporeAirport.shtml.*

on core competence and outsource peripheral activities) does not readily apply. External suppliers would not be able to offer the value that SIA's own subsidiaries can offer to SIA. This kind of related diversification leads to the benefits of strategic synergy in terms of reliability of key inputs, high quality, transfer of learning as well as cost-effectiveness.

Bringing It All Together: Building a Self-Reinforcing Activity System

How specifically do these elements lead to cost-effective service excellence? Figure 3–5 shows how. The five pillars of SIA's cost-effective service excellence are supported, operationalized and

Figure 3–5

SIA's self-reinforcing activity system for developing cost-effective service excellence

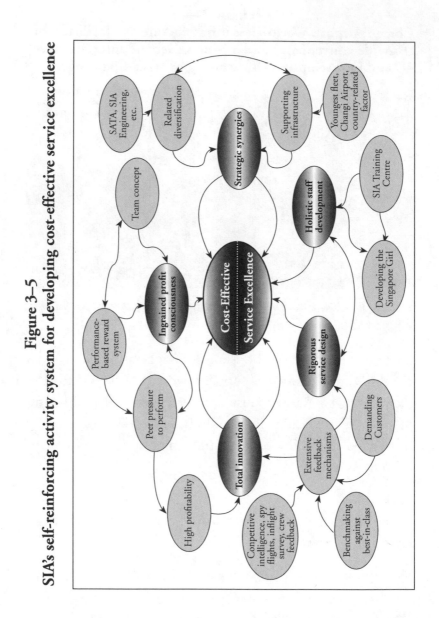

made real to everyday decisions and actions through a self-reinforcing activity system of virtuous circles. The cultural values of cost-effective service excellence are thus more than just abstract ideas. They are ingrained in both the minds of employees and the organizational processes. This may help explain why SIA's competitive advantage has been sustained for decades. While it is easy to copy single elements, it is much harder to reproduce an entire, and self-reinforcing, activity system. Even so, complacency is an enemy that is continually banished from SIA in favour of continuous improvement in delivering cost-effective service excellence.

The Emergence of Biometrics

SIA's employment of biometric technology in pursuit of its core competence of cost-effective service excellence illustrates the pillars of rigorous service design and development along with total innovation.

Intense competitive pressures and razor-thin margins in the airline industry, as in many other industries, do not allow firms the luxury of freely expending resources to improve service. Rather, the trick is to constantly seek ways to achieve leaps in service quality as well as efficiency simultaneously. Internet technology has in the last few years allowed many firms to do just that, and it has redefined several service-oriented industries, such as retail financial services, insurance services, book and music retailing, and travel agencies. Biometrics may be the next major technology after the Internet that enables further value and productivity enhancements for those firms that know how to harness its power.

Biometrics is the authentication or identification[8] of

individuals based on a physiological or behavioural characteristic. Physiological characteristics include fingerprints, facial recognition, hand geometry or iris configuration, while behavioural traits include signature, keystroke and voice patterns. Biometrics, as something you *are*, is both more convenient and more secure than something you *know* (passwords or personal information) or something you *have* (card keys, smart cards or tokens). There is no risk of forgetting, losing, duplicating, loaning or getting your biometrics stolen, especially if a multi-biometric approach is used for authentication. The dominant security enhancement technology leaves a lot to be desired. It has been estimated that between half to a third of calls for technical assistance are password related and that the cost of managing multiple passwords and resetting passwords ranges from US$200 to US$340 per employee per year.[9] The cost of administering external customers' passwords is also significant.

Biometrics can offer significant improvement to security enhancement processes as well as other value-added applications. Potential applications of biometric technology range from controlling physical access to facilities (used by Disney World to provide access to season-pass holders) and enabling voice recognition at call centres (used by the Home Shopping Network and Charles Schwab to enable hassle-free client authentication) to controlling the time and attendance of employees (used by McDonald's), providing self-service access to safe deposit vaults at banks (used by the Bank of Hawaii) and cashing cheques in supermarkets (used by Kroger).

Security concerns and the rising incidence and sophistication of fraud, such as identity theft, combined with advances in biometric technology and declining costs have provided an impetus for greater diffusion of biometrics and highlighted immense potential. While in 2003 the biometrics industry's revenues were US$719 million, in 2004 they were US$1.44 billion, and they are expected to rise to at least US$4.6 billon by 2008. Currently, the lion's share of biometric technologies is accounted for by fingerprint identification at 48%, followed by face recognition at 12% and hand geometry at 11%. Iris recognition, by far the most secure method but which costs considerably more to implement and has a lower level of customer acceptance, has a 9% market share.[10]

However, the overwhelming majority of current biometrics uses are focused on simply improving security rather than on providing quantum leaps to customer service improvement while simultaneously raising efficiency and security. The winners of tomorrow will be firms that manage to harness the power of biometrics to achieve this essential combination.

Outperforming an Extremely Tough Industry

We spoke to SIA, arguably one of the most successful innovators and service leaders in its industry, and the Civil Aviation Authority of Singapore (CAAS), the operator of arguably the best airport in the world,[11] on their current thinking on biometrics and how they are using this technology to fulfil every traveller's dream when it comes to airport procedures: the ability to breeze through airline check-in, security checks as well as immigration checks in less than one minute, all within a context of enhanced travel security.

SIA and CAAS believe that, in line with technological trends and international developments, in the near future most international travellers will carry a passport, visa or smart card which will contain selected biometric information on its owner. In response to this trend, a task force in SIA has identified an astounding 113 potential biometrics applications and is currently exploring which ones would provide simultaneously strategic differentiation through service excellence and improvement in productivity, cost-effectiveness as well as security.

The two strategies of focusing on value-added differentiation through premium quality on the one hand and focusing on system-wide efficiency and aiming for cost leadership on the other, have been seen as incompatible, since they can entail mutually contradictory actions at the operational level. It has been argued that any such combination of incompatible generic strategies would at best be temporary and risk getting the company stuck in the middle, having neither high levels of differentiation nor sustainable low costs.[12] In spite of arguments to the contrary,[13] successfully achieving a combination of differentiation and cost-effectiveness has been rare.

One organization that have achieved this is SIA. Our studies have shown that SIA has provided for decades premium levels of quality and innovation while at the same time maintaining lower costs than its peers. This has enabled SIA to consistently outperform the airline industry, a key measure of robust sustainable competitive advantage. It has achieved this in an industry that is extremely tough to compete in, given its disastrous business cycles, overcapacity, difficulty of differentiation and high-risk profile.[14] Figure 3–6 compares the performance of SIA against the weighted average of the world's top 20 airlines for the five years from 1999 to 2003.

Figure 3–6
SIA versus the top 20 airlines by market capitalization

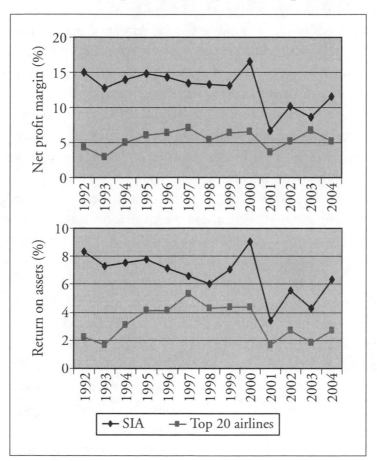

Note: The top 20 airlines (as of 15 May 2004) were Southwest Airlines, SIA, Cathay Pacific, Japan Airlines, Lufthansa, British Airways, All Nippon Airways, Qantas, Air France, Ryanair, JetBlue Airways, China Southern Airlines (A shares), China Eastern Airlines (A shares), Thai Airways, American Airlines, Malaysia Airlines, SAS AB, China Airlines, WestJet Airlines and Alitalia.

The Advent of Fully Automated Seamless Travel

Two significant applications of biometric technology are currently being developed at SIA's hub at Changi Airport in Singapore: the FAST (fully automated seamless travel) process and the baggage drop-off system. In November 2004, a six-month pilot test of FAST was initiated that integrates three processes: airline check-in, pre-immigration security checks and immigration clearance. This will eliminate the hassle of going through these procedures separately (Figure 3–7). Most biometrics-based trials elsewhere primarily focus on improving security, are limited to specific processes or areas (such as access control to secured areas, airline check-in or immigration checks), and at the implementation level apply mostly to airport staff or a limited number of selected frequent flyers rather than a broad spectrum of passengers. This initiative at Changi Airport is a world's first of integrating these processes with the clear objective of driving service excellence in airport operations and SIA's ground services while at the same time enhancing efficiency and security. FAST is expected to be rolled out in the near future to serve all passengers who carry biometric cards and all airlines operating through Changi Airport. In addition to improving security, FAST aims to serve the additional purpose of delivering great customer service and convenience as well as reducing airline and airport costs by simplifying procedures, reducing error and making efficient use of self-service technology (see Figure 3–8).

The pilot phase, implemented at Terminal 2 of Changi Airport, involves 9,000 of SIA's frequent flyers who are Singapore citizens. Participants first sign up at an enrolment station of the Immigration and Checkpoints Authority, where

Figure 3–7
Traditional immigration checks will be history with the
introduction of hassle-free multi-biometric systems

Source: *www.asiatraveltips.com/PicturesofSingaporeAirport.shtml.*

their biometric information (fingerprints and facial features)
is captured on a smart card called SVIP (smart visa for
identification with passport). When travelling, these registered
users can simply walk through a separate gateway at immigration, where they can do a self-service check-in at a computer-
ized service station. Here, they tap their card on a reader, have
their fingerprint scanned, and check in with the help of a touch
screen while their face is being scanned by a camera. The system
identifies the card holder, clears security checks and immigration, recommends a seat based on the known preferences of
the traveller and, upon acceptance of the seat by the traveller,

Figure 3–8
Carting heavy luggage in the departure hall will be a thing
of the past with the proposed baggage drop-off

Source: *ww.asiatraveltips.com/PicturesofSingaporeAirport.shtml.*

prints a boarding pass. If the traveller is happy with the suggested seat, the entire process takes less than 60 seconds, down from a current average of (already highly efficient) 8–15 minutes. If the passenger changes the choice of seat three times (the cabin seating with available seats is displayed on the check-in touch screen), the time needed for the entire process could rise to 3 minutes. The pilot test does not handle passengers with check-in baggage, but a separate process is being considered for that. Hand luggage is taken on board as usual.

The FAST pilot technology is integrated with a number of existing systems. The first is SIA's booking system for processing seating preferences and real-time seat allocation and confirmation. Another is Singapore's current immigration automated clearance system used at the border between Singapore and Malaysia to facilitate immigration clearance for the tens of thousands of daily commuters travelling to and from Malaysia who live in one of the two countries and work in the other. The system monitors entry and exit from Singapore and checks traveller details against those in the immigration databases. The third is the SVIP card, an initiative by the Singapore Ministry of Home Affairs to meet US immigration requirements.

The FAST process looks simple from the customer's perspective, as it should, but it is in fact highly complex from a legal, security and technological perspective, which makes it extremely difficult to imitate by competing airlines and airports. The development and piloting of FAST requires close cooperation among five organizations, each with their own priorities, concerns and systems. The organizations are SIA, CAAS, the Immigration and Checkpoints Authority, the Singapore Police Force and the Ministry of Home Affairs. The pilot uses a multi-biometric approach, combining facial recognition, preferred by the European Union, and finger-printing, preferred by Singapore's authorities and currently employed in the immigration automated clearance system at the border with Malaysia. One consideration in developing the system was the aim of meeting the requirements of the US Enhanced Border Security and Visa Entry Reform Act of 2002.

Besides harmonizing with European Union and US standards, this multi-biometic approach helps minimize the two key error indicators of biometric identification systems: the false rejection rate, which refers to the right person being rejected and would cause inconvenience to that person until his or her identity is established, and the false acceptance rate, which refers to the wrong person being identified as a legitimate card or visa holder and allowed to travel and is thus a more critical indicator for security purposes. To align with European Union privacy laws, no biometric data is stored at the airport or elsewhere. Rather, all data is stored on the passenger's own smart card. In the event of card loss, unauthorized alteration of the data stored on that card would be virtually impossible since it is protected by a complex algorithm and the keys are kept by Singapore's Immigration and Checkpoints Authority.

Different service processes have different security needs. For example, a 99% accuracy of a voice recognition application may be a quantum leap of improvement for caller identification in a call centre that is currently identifying customers through their stored telephone numbers. For immigration processes, however, accuracy levels cannot be compromised and 99% would be unacceptable. In such cases, multi-biometric systems can be used, as in FAST or in the US-VISIT programme, where inbound travellers' index fingers are scanned and their photos taken upon arrival in the US.

Another application of biometrics being considered is a baggage drop-off system. Currently, all passengers with check-in baggage have to go through the inconvenience of carrying their bags to the check-in counter from the vehicle they arrived in (Figure 3–8). The idea proposes to eliminate this inconvenience by allowing passengers to drop off their baggage outside the building as soon as they come out of the vehicle. The baggage drop-off idea clearly complements the biometrics-based check-in process, which in its current form can only handle passengers with hand luggage.

The above innovations are taking place in the context of Singapore's strategic objective of maintaining and improving its hub status in the region, given its importance to the country's sustained economic growth and its reputation as a paragon of efficiency. The relevant organizations are currently considering how to employ the smart card in commercial applications to enhance travellers' convenience when they are in Singapore. SIA and CAAS will be carefully monitoring customer satisfaction, system reliability, and efficiency during the trial and will fine-tune and improve the system before it is rolled out to all travellers and all airlines using Changi Airport.

Sustaining Competitive Advantage through Biometrics

As the preceding discussion suggests, the challenge is to move beyond incremental applications of biometrics focusing simply on security to consciously designing applications that aim at combining service excellence with higher efficiency, where higher security is a by-product of this process rather than the raison d'etre. This entails thinking both about how to enhance the customer experience and about designing and implementing significant process reconfigurations, as Figure 3–9 shows.

Figure 3–9
Achieving sustainable advantage through the use of biometric technology

	Small-scale process improvement	Significant process reconfiguration
Significant	Voice recognition, bank transaction authorization, electronic point of sale, secure operation of automated teller machines or bank vaults	Sustainable, differentiating market offerings (e.g., FAST)
Negligible or incremental	Control of employee access to airports, laboratories or government facilities, user access to secure computer networks, time and attendance at work	National immigration processing (e.g., US-VISIT), management of patient records in healthcare institutions, control of state benefits fraud

Potential impact on user/customer experience

Extent of business process redesign

The lower left quadrant includes examples of biometric applications that neither involve significant business process redesign nor present the potential for value-added customer or user experience. The lower right quadrant shows examples involving significant process reconfigurations but still without the potential for substantial value added to customers or users. These two quadrants primarily focus on control such as controlling access, attendance or entry. The upper left quadrant consists of applications that offer the potential for improving the customer experience, but they can easily be copied by competitors because these improvements do not involve significant business process reconfiguration. As a result, these applications have become, or are on the way to becoming, essential in order to compete; they are hygiene factors rather than differentiators. Locating oneself in the top right quadrant, on the other hand, can provide a sustainable advantage, since the innovations offered and the related customer experience are supported by unique and internally coherent operational configurations that have a long lead time, involve specialist knowledge, and presuppose tight interwoven systems and close coordination among the employees and other stakeholders involved in the process.[15]

Unleashing Future Potential

We could not locate another example of harnessing biometric technology to the same extent as FAST to offer service excellence, improve efficiency as well as increase security in other service industries, and we foresee that it will be several years before something similar is offered in the aviation industry itself.

Our research at SIA and CAAS has convinced us that one of the forthcoming quantum leaps in differentiation via service innovation in the airline industry is the full-fledged integration of biometrics with several customer service, security and immigration processes to provide a seamless, hassle-free, safe and convenient travel experience. This is not simply an application of new technology to make existing processes faster but one to radically reengineer these processes. This is only the beginning for SIA and CAAS. In addition to FAST and the baggage drop-off concept, other ideas that may be realized and integrated in the near future include access control to airport lounges, issuing and payment of tickets, loyalty programme service processes and voice recognition at call centres. Some of these applications can be copied by competitors on a stand-alone basis, but their overall and mutually reinforcing effects cannot.

The unique combination of SIA and Changi Airport as innovation-driven service leaders together with a forward-looking and competitively oriented leadership in Singapore (often referred to as Singapore Inc.) allows us to catch a glimpse of the potential biometrics can offer to service firms more broadly. It is only a matter of time before imaginative applications follow in other industries, made possible by more people around the world carrying smart cards (which could be, for example, integrated into credit cards) or biometric identification documents such as passports, identity cards or driving licences. The field is open for competitors to claim the high ground and achieve sustainable success by effectively using the emerging technology of biometrics.

Technology advances combined with creative minds in many service organizations do not allow us to predict accurately which biometric service applications will eventually become the 'killer' applications and how, but it appears certain that it is only a matter of time before biometrics revolutionizes service delivery and allows service firms to realize significant gains in service quality, customer convenience, safety and productivity, all at the same time.

In Conclusion

In this chapter, we have addressed SIA's core competence – cost-effective service excellence – and concluded that SIA has managed to consistently deliver service excellence in an efficient manner as well as to successfully incorporate an integrated cost leadership and differentiation strategy. In addition to exhibiting the key characteristics of leading service organizations, such as management commitment, customer-focused staff and systems, and a customer-oriented culture, SIA has achieved success through the five pillars that constitute its unique activity system: rigorous service design and development, total innovation that integrates continuous incremental improvements with discontinuous major innovations, profit and cost consciousness ingrained in all employees, holistic staff development, and reaping of strategic synergies through related diversification and a world-class infrastructure. These five pillars of SIA's cost-effective service excellence are supported, operationalized and made real to everyday decisions and actions through a self-reinforcing and sustainable activity system of virtuous circles.

We then discussed SIA's investment in biometrics, which illustrates its pillars of rigorous service design and development and total innovation, and proposed that sustaining competitive advantage through the strategic use of technology, including biometrics, involves developing innovations that have a significant positive impact on the customer experience and also entails significant business process redesign, which will make the innovations difficult to imitate.

NOTES

This chapter draws from L. Heracleous, J. Wirtz and R. Johnston, 'Cost effective service excellence: Lessons from Singapore Airlines', *Business Strategy Review*, Spring 2004, pp. 33–8; Heracleous and Wirtz, *Biometrics: The Next Frontier in Service Excellence, Productivity and Security, Managing Service Quality*, Spring 2006 (forthcoming) and Wirtz and Heracleous, 'Biometrics meets services', *Harvard Business Review*, February 2005, p. 48.

[1]   'About SIA', *www.singaporeair.com.*

[2]   Ian Batey, *Asian Branding: A Great Way to Fly*, Singapore: Prentice Hall, 2002, p. 123.

[3]   M. Porter, *Competitive Advantage*, New York: Free Press, 1985.

[4]   Batey, p. 120.

[5]   G. L. Shostack, 'Designing services that deliver', *Harvard Business Review*, 62, no. 1 (1984): 133–9.

[6]   Batey, p. 136.

[7]   In addition to the named quotations, this section draws on in-depth interviews with Choo Poh Leong (Senior Manager, Crew Services) and Toh Giam Ming (Senior Manager, Crew Performance).

[8]   Authentication is a 1-to-1 comparison to essentially answer the question "Are you who you say you are?"; identification is a more complex process of a 1-to-n comparison to answer the question "Who are you?"

[9]   *www.Forrester.com, www.Gartner.com.*

[10]   International Biometrics Group, *www.biometricgroup.com.*

[11]   'Changi Airport snaps up six awards in September', *International Travel Daily News*, 27 September 2004, *www.traveldailynews.com.*

[12]   M. E. Porter, *"Competitive Strategy: Techniques for Analyzing Industries and Competitors*, New York: Free Press, 1980.

13   See, e.g., C. W. Hill, 'Differentiation versus low cost or differentiation and low cost: A contingency framework', *Academy of Management Review*, 13 (1988): 401–12.

14   D. S. Harned, P. R. Costa and J. T. Lundquist, 'Rethinking the aviation industry', *McKinsey Quarterly*, Risk and Resilience Special Issue (2002): 89–100.

15   See, e.g., M. E. Porter, 'What is strategy?', *Harvard Business Review*, November–December 1996, pp. 61–78.

THE SKY IS NOW ONLINE.

Broadband internet will soon be available in every seat in every class, connecting you to the world. You can surf, email and for the first time, watch real time TV news on your laptop*. It's yet another addition to the inflight service even other airlines talk about.
www.singaporeair.com

connexion

SINGAPORE AIRLINES

4

Innovation as a Key to Sustained Service Excellence

This chapter explores the role of service innovation in enabling SIA to sustain cost-effective service excellence for over three decades. We begin by presenting SIA senior management's perspective of the key challenges the airline faces in delivering sustained cost-effective service excellence. Our research has shown that SIA's main approaches to these challenges are mostly related to constant innovation, service redesign and new-service development. Therefore, the rest of the chapter will focus on

SIA's approaches to innovation and shed light on SIA's ability as a serial innovator, introducing many firsts in the airline industry over the years and sustaining this innovative orientation over decades in the face of intense cost pressures, industry crises and the push towards commoditization. The company's approach involves the seamless combination of hard, structured, rigorous and centralized innovation on the one hand and soft, emergent and distributed innovation on the other.

The Key Challenges of Delivering Service Excellence

Three key challenges SIA faces stood out in our interviews with its senior management. It is important to understand these challenges to be able to appreciate the drive behind SIA's innovation capability. These three key challenges are as follows:

- How to consistently satisfy the sky-high and still rising expectations of its demanding customer base
- How to balance standardization and personalization of its services and overcome the tension between these two needs
- How to approach a large number of services in totality to attain excellence in all processes and supporting subprocesses

Dealing with sky-high and ever-rising customer expectations

Having an international reputation for service excellence actually makes delivering outstanding service a continuous challenge, because customers tend to adjust their expectations according to the reputation and brand image of the company. Yap Kim Wah, Senior Vice President (Product and Service), explains: "We have a high reputation for service and that means when someone flies with us they come with high expectations. Still, we want them to say 'Wow! That is something out of the ordinary'."

Furthermore, customers' expectations are also influenced by the service standards of other airlines as well as of service firms in other industries. Hence, SIA works at not only being the best in the airline industry but also being the best service company. Mr Yap adds, "This is a fantastic challenge for us. We have to look at everything we do. This means, for instance, the food we serve on board, and our food and beverage service, has to be the best. So we serve the best champagne; and even when we serve local dishes such as chicken rice, they have to be the best in the local market. If we can't achieve this with a dish, we would just have to drop the item."

In order to deliver an extraordinary service that delights even customers with high expectations, SIA attaches considerable importance to the 'wow' effect, as Mr Yap explains, "It's the new things that create the 'wow'. The things that customers never expected. There is a whole realm of things that customers don't know they want! We try to study the trends. We have a product innovation department that continuously looks at trends, why people behave in a certain manner and why they do certain things. And then we do a projection over three to five years. We try to follow both short- and long-

term trends." Besides trends analysis, SIA also uses feedback from its staff, information about other airlines, customer compliment/complaint analysis and major traveller
surveys to help it generate new ideas. The new ideas
gathered from the various sources enable the airline to
constantly identify all possible opportunities to delight its
customers through the introduction of new services, such as
its direct flyer from Singapore to Los Angeles which required
significant service innovation for this extremely long flight
(Figure 4–1).

Figure 4–1
SIA's direct flyer to Los Angeles: A world's first for ultra long haul flights

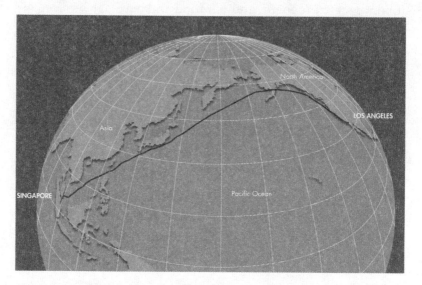

Courtesy of Singapore Airlines.

Mr Yap adds, "It's very easy to be contend with what we do, and that's the danger. It's easy to say that customers will surely want what we are doing now. To be a winner, however, we have to continually strive to provide the very best service when compared with any industry. That's why it's so challenging. Whatever we do, we are in search of excellence and are never willing to settle for what we have already achieved. Moreover, although it's good to be passionate about a product, I think one must be willing to kill it with a product in x number of months. It could be 6 months, it could be 12 months, it could be 20 months. But you have got to kill it because the lifestyles of our customers are continuously evolving. This requires constant innovation and constant development in all the things that we do." Clearly, SIA sees constant innovation as the key to addressing the sky-high and ever-rising expectations of its passengers.

Balancing standardization and customization of service

According to Sim Kay Wee, formerly Senior Vice President (Cabin Crew), "The challenge in service is that there has to be consistency. When you buy a product, it's very different from buying a service. If you buy a piece of soap, for example, it's just a piece of soap, manufactured by the same process day in and day out. A service, however, is more human, with the potential for inconsistency." Yet, SIA would not want its passengers to experience different service standards on different trips. It wants to ensure that its passengers will get the same consistent level of excellent service on every trip. To achieve consistency, all new procedures are finely honed and tested before any change is introduced.

While all the components of a service are important, there is a crucial difference between hygiene factors and enhancing factors. Mr Sim explains, "We have a long list of the things that passengers expect of good service: convenient flight schedules, punctuality, seat comfort and technical aspects such as safety, or even skills such as pouring a cup of coffee without spilling it all over the place. But those are just technical, and I think a lot of airlines can master them. These are all hygiene factors that you must have. Mind you, there are some airlines that don't have them and are still in business! The enhancing factors are the softer skills, such as warmth, care and anticipation of needs." SIA's strategy is to ensure that hygiene factors, which are expected by most travellers, are consistently delivered, while the enhancing factors are personalized and show more variance. It aims to give service that is personalized to the needs of each individual, especially in the premium classes.

The biggest challenge in delivering consistent yet personalized service comes from the people. Mr Sim explains, "The additional complication is that, while striving for consistency, we need people who can be flexible. I know this is a contradiction, but the worst thing about service delivery is when everybody just follows the book. We want them to be flexible and creative. In Singapore, there is a tendency for people to be too regimented in their thinking. If a passenger asks for a vegetarian meal and we do not have it on board, for example, we want the member of staff to go back to the galley, think on the spot and create a solution, such as putting together a plate from all the fruits and vegetables, rather than telling the customer that it is not catered for and so he can't have it."

In order to manage this constant struggle of offering standardized service that is at the same time personalized, SIA also places a great deal of emphasis on the testing of all procedures to ensure that they can be consistently delivered and on the participation of all employees from all levels in the innovation processes so as to foster creativity and flexibility. This is important because when the staff have mastered the basic processes they will then have the capacity to watch out for opportunities to personalize, to anticipate needs and to regularly create the 'wow' effect that will surprise and delight customers instead of merely satisfying them. In short, careful attention to the implementation and operations issues of new services and processes is seen as crucial to SIA's ability to straddle the easily conflicting goals of standardization and customization of service delivery.

Attaining excellence in all processes and subprocesses

Recognizing that customers are buying the total travel experience, service excellence to SIA means that all its service components have to be excellent: everything that the customer will encounter during the journey and even before that, all processes and subprocesses, ranging from reservation and ground services, to inflight services, food and beverages, seats and foot rests, as well as services related to its frequent flyer programme. Mr Yap illustrates, "A flight has many, many subcomponents. Being better at every one of these subcomponents will give our competitors a hard time. By the time they copy them, we would already have moved ahead. This requires constant innovation and constant development in all the things we do. We don't just put the best seats in business class and sit back. We want to provide the best inflight service, the best food, the best service on the ground, besides the best seats." Summarizing SIA's perspective on totality, he continues, "It is better to be 1% better in 100 things than 100% better in one thing."

To provide a service that is excellent in all aspects and that surpasses its competitors' in many areas is a challenge, as many people and much technology are involved in the numerous main and subprocesses. Precisely this complexity, however, allows SIA to gain a competitive edge through its focus on totality. The airline needs to constantly improve its processes and subprocesses to maintain this edge as well as to keep pace with customers' changing needs and expectations.

SIA's focus on totality extends to its approach to launching new services. It makes sure that its launches are conducted as complete and integrated packages because, as Mr Yap explains, "It is a stronger proposition to our customers than saying we have a new and better cup. We say that the cup comes with better coffee, better service and a better design."

The SIA Approach to Continuous Improvement and New-Service Development

SIA's approaches to overcoming its key challenges in delivering sustained service excellence are in one way or another all linked to constant innovation and improvement. We believe that it is the company's strong innovation capability that has enabled it to sustain service excellence and secure its service leadership position over decades. Unlike many other service firms, which tend to rely heavily on centralized research and development departments to develop new services, SIA's approach to new-service development involves the seamless combination of hard, structured, rigorous and centralized innovation, headed mainly by the product innovation department, with soft, emergent, distributed but equally significant innovation, carried out mainly by the various functional departments.

The airline appreciates the importance of regularly introducing discontinuous, major innovations that amaze and position it as a service leader in the eyes of its passengers. Such innovations may be the first on-demand inflight entertainment system for all travel classes or the flat bed in business class, as shown in Figure 4–2. At the same time, it is also necessary to continuously churn out incremental, cost-effective innovations across all its operating units to ensure constant improvement of its service standards, as well as productivity. These distributed innovations produced by the individual functional departments give SIA an edge over its competitors and help it sustain high standards for all the components of its service. To SIA, innovation is not just about coming up with new ideas but also about looking at old ideas and thinking about how to make them better. Hence, sustaining service excellence through constant innovation is not so much about employing creative minds and getting them to innovate, it is more about encouraging the staff to constantly look at all the processes to search for opportunities to improve.

Figure 4–2
The business class: 'Spacebed' allowing the passenger
more space to work and relax and to sleep in a flat position

Courtesy of Singapore Airlines.

The result is a small improvement each time, but that occurs
all the time and in all areas, making it very difficult for
competitors to catch up. We will next discuss SIA's centralized
new-service design capabilities before turning to its distributed
innovation capabilities.

The Centralized Innovation Approach to Designing Major Service Breakthroughs

Undertaken by the product innovation department, the
equivalent of the product development department in other
companies, centralized innovation involves mainly 'hard' and

highly structured and mostly major, discontinuous innovations, such as the recently launched non-stop service between Singapore and New York with upgraded business and 'executive economy' classes (Figure 4–3) or the design of the Airbus A380 cabin. The product innovation department consists of a small group of people whose key task is to conceive innovative ideas and take selected ones through the development cycle to commercial introduction.

Figure 4–3
The new executive economy class cabin affording extra comfort on SIA's ultralong-haul flights between Singapore and America

Courtesy of Singapore Airlines.

The department follows a well-defined innovation framework guiding its activities, which involves new-service development processes such as opportunity identification and selection, concept evaluation, design and development, and new-service launches. At the preliminary stage, there must be abundant useful information that provides valuable insights on where to start. The information can come from various sources, including performance benchmarking surveys conducted by IATA, surveys conducted with random samples of passengers on about 10% of SIA's flights, focus groups and feedback. After the opportunities have been identified, evaluated and then approved by the management committee, design, development and finally launch follow (see Figure 4–4).

Figure 4–4
SIA's three-step centralized innovation process

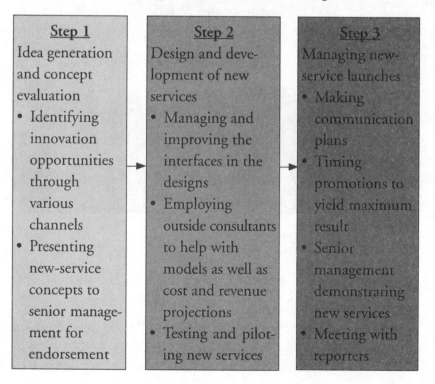

<u>Step 1</u>	<u>Step 2</u>	<u>Step 3</u>
Idea generation and concept evaluation	Design and development of new services	Managing new-service launches
• Identifying innovation opportunities through various channels	• Managing and improving the interfaces in the designs	• Making communication plans
• Presenting new-service concepts to senior management for endorsement	• Employing outside consultants to help with models as well as cost and revenue projections	• Timing promotions to yield maximum result
	• Testing and piloting new services	• Senior management demonstrating new services
		• Meeting with reporters

SIA's innovation is heavily driven by customer needs. According to Mr Yap, "SIA is a profit-oriented organization. We are not an institute of technology. Whatever we do must make business sense and that is the guiding principle. To support the guiding principle that we have to make a profit and customers must want to return, all innovations, in one way or another, must be something that customers need, although sometimes customers may not know what they need!"

Idea generation and concept evaluation

The product innovation department relies on various sources of information for new ideas, such as examining lifestyle trends and competitor analyses, surfing the Internet, attending conferences, gathering feedback from front-line staff and customers, and consulting with designers worldwide.

SIA closely monitors the competition. By looking at what the competitors are or are not offering, SIA gains a better knowledge of what might work for SIA. A research department has been set up to track competitors' as well as SIA's products and services. This tracking allows SIA to explore the needs that are not yet or not fully satisfied by existing service offerings. Whenever a competitor offers a new service, SIA would send its people to try it out. It would then make an assessment to see if it should introduce the new service as well, and if yes, if it should come up with something that is better. To track the competition more closely, SIA subscribes to an IATA market research tool called GAP (Global Airlines Performance) survey. From this survey, it identifies airlines with significant improvements or those that are particularly strong in certain aspects. Those are the airlines it will study in depth to see what can be learned from them.

In order to sustain a competitive advantage, SIA constantly benchmarks itself against its competitors to make sure that it is always slightly ahead of them. According to Dr Yeoh Teng Kwong, formerly Senior Manager (Product Innovation), "Innovation does not necessarily mean always coming up with new ideas ourselves. If somebody can do something very well, we can emulate them and do better if we can." For instance, SIA was not the first to adopt Boeing Connection, as it had already been on trial on Lufthansa, SAS and Delta. However, SIA saw the potential in it and looked for ways it can differentiate the new service in terms of application, content and other functions.

However, it is insufficient to take competitors' innovations and improve on them. Real differentiating ideas are needed in order for SIA to secure its service leadership position because, ultimately, it is the brand new ideas that will produce the 'wow' effect. Mr Yap explains, "Idea generation within SIA is, to a large extent, governed by the need to differentiate – in other words, staying ahead – as we are a premium carrier. Therefore, there will always be ideas that we come up with that are uniquely different from those of others."

Although the product innovation department's main task is to churn out major and substantial innovations, it also has a 'soft', flexible and unstructured innovation process to allow individuals in that department to pursue less orthodox ideas. These ideas, if they have potential, may later go through the formal new-service development process or be passed to the operational units for development. Additionally, to encourage employees to actively participate in the opportunity identification process, all employees have a chance to be selected to take part in a programme known as Future Works. Future Works is like an annual mini boot camp that brings together some 50 executives from various departments to do brainstorming. The participants will have a chance to let their imagination run wild. At the end of the workshop, they will present their ideas to the venture board, a selected group of SIA senior vice presidents. Funds will be provided to develop ideas that the board endorses.

There is also a very simple innovation system called a central electronic log which allows everyone, from all levels, in the product innovation department to participate and contribute to innovation. Whenever members of the department find any exciting new idea or technology from the Internet, newspapers or elsewhere, they are encouraged to capture the idea in the electronic log. At any one time, the log has about 20 to 30 ideas, many of which are wild and preliminary. Meetings are held every few weeks to discuss the ideas logged.

In general, SIA has been successful in getting employees from all levels to participate and contribute to the idea and concept generation process. This is partly because it has successfully instilled a culture, and set up the processes, that encourages staff to contribute ideas. Dr Yeoh adds, "Innovation is not really about getting a bunch of geniuses to sit down together and think of ideas. Instead, SIA makes innovation possible and easy by using the oxymoron called 'systematic innovation'."

Design and development of innovations

After identifying and selecting innovative ideas, and receiving the endorsement of the management committee, a new innovation has to be carefully developed before it can add real value to SIA and its passengers. Development consists of the creation of everything from the design to the marketing concept of a new service.

As the customer's interest is always SIA's top priority, much time is devoted to ensuring that any innovation is extremely user-friendly. Various models and combinations are tried out and subjected to thorough testing. According to Timothy Chua, Senior Manager of Inflight Services (Projects), "We focus very much on simplicity and ease of use, constantly reviewing existing steps and eliminating steps where necessary to make it as simple as possible. Ultimately, if we have something that's not easy to use, it doesn't serve the intended purpose."

SIA also brings in outside consultants to help with the modelling and projections for more complex products. A consulting firm was roped in to assist in the development of the Airbus A380 cabin concepts using various analytical tools, including conjoint and financial analyses, to help optimize the cabin design, including such tricky issues as the seat count in the cabin. Outside consultants are also engaged to verify and validate the ideas, processes and numbers developed by SIA staff in order to obtain more neutral, potentially less biased or different views.

Because of the cross-functional nature of airline operations, the right mix of people should be present on a new-service development team. Dr Yeoh reveals that the senior staff in the product innovation department tend to be the project drivers, but each team has roughly equal numbers of people from relevant departments to ensure a cross-functional perspective to a project.

After the product development proposals have been drawn up, much time will be spent on fine-tuning and identifying potential failure points by asking what can go wrong and why. All the different potential failure points will be connected to get a coherent picture of the underlying problems, and work then begins on addressing them. Testing and piloting come after the design and engineering stages. Instead of investing considerable capital in large-scale implementations, SIA prefers to conduct small trials, often with a small group of priority customers, to test a new service.

Managing new-service launches

Somewhere along the process, after all the piloting, testing and trials, if management is convinced that the new service should be introduced, it will be marketed to customers. In order to encourage the adoption of a new service and to increase its usage, SIA engages in promotional activities which they call spot promotions. During the initial launches, it holds media events in which a member of senior management meets with reporters and demonstrates a new service. After the initial launches, SIA often runs various types of promotions, including lucky draws and double frequent flyer points (Figure 4–5), to encourage customer adoption. New services recently promoted included a new check-in service based on SMS (short message service), e-mail and Internet services for the frequent flyer programme, and online redemption of frequent flyer rewards. This final phase of new-service management is important as customers need to be educated about the benefits of the new service and how it operates in order to facilitate customer adoption.

Figure 4–5
Greater convenience and earning double mileage for passengers flying to Amritsar, India, within the promotional period

Source: *Priority Quarterly Magazine*, 4th quarter 2004.

The Distributed Innovation Approach to Continuous Improvement and Major Redesign of Processes throughout the Organization

Besides the centralized hard approach, there is also a softer new-service development process in SIA, which can perhaps best be described as distributed innovation that truly differentiates the company's innovation and new-service development approaches from those of many other companies. Unlike centralized innovation, which is undertaken by the product innovation department and follows a well-defined framework involving a number of key fixed stages (e.g., initial senior management endorsement, development of a robust business case and senior management approval), distributed innovation is under individual functional departments. It is primarily an unstructured, emergent process that focuses on continuous improvement and tends to be more fluid and flexible. The budget for distributed innovation is often absorbed into the individual departments' operating expenses. As explained by Dr Yeoh, "I would not consider the product innovation department as the central product development unit, as this would give the impression that it drives all new developments in SIA. Far from it, the culture of innovation is so pervasive in the company that most functional departments have the innovation objective as part of their mission. SIA strives to excel in a multitude of areas so that our competitors find it a near-insurmountable task to try to rival us."

SIA's culture encourages a stream of new ideas from its various functions, such as inflight services, ground services and loyalty marketing. These ideas are developed and implemented by the people in those functions in a decentralized, distributed manner, using department budgets at least for the initial stages of development. The recently redesigned Internet check-in service, which built on the acceptance and high utilization of the telephone and SMS check-in services, was conceptualized, developed and implemented by the ground services department. Distributed innovation is especially important in sustaining the aspect of service excellence that requires all the components of a service encounter to be excellent, as it helps ensure that all functional departments focus on improving their respective services.

This fluid process also enables and encourages continuous monitoring and further development based on staff and customer feedback of innovations that specific departments own. Continuous enhancement of the SMS check-in process has been made to improve its functionality without sacrificing ease of use. Other improvements which have resulted from distributed innovation include the now commonly offered facility to choose one's seat through the Internet or SMS and the unique book-the-cook service that allows business- and first-class passengers to order their favourite dish before taking their flight.

This distributed innovation capability offers another advantage guarding against the blind pursuit of technological fads, as it involves the people who are close to the actual processes and who therefore can more easily identify what will work. During the height of the WAP (wireless application protocol) hype, the ground services department made a conscious decision, to forgo this technology in favour of SMS check-in, because SMS was considered more user-friendly and it was readily available to most of its passengers.

In addition, the direct involvement of operations in the innovation process means that the ability to consistently and seamlessly deliver service, a cornerstone of SIA's success, is not compromised by the introduction of innovations that sound good but cannot be delivered reliably in the air or on the ground. The proposal to let passengers order inflight drinks through the inflight entertainment system, Krisflyer, was dropped, because it would be difficult to deliver the drinks to passengers with the necessary level of customization within a reasonable time. This operational ownership of innovations at the departmental level is crucial for SIA, reinforcing its key competency, which is the operational ability to deliver consistent and reliable service every time, in every customer transaction.

This soft distributed process also has a 'hard' edge. Although major, discontinuous innovations are usually undertaken by the product innovation department, functional departments also undertake the development of major new services that fall mainly within their area of control. While minor adjustments can be made almost anytime, the more expensive and significant changes are subjected to similar key fixed development stages as practised by the product innovation department (e.g., senior management endorsement, costing and approval). However, these developments are carried out independently of the product innovation department and are generally overseen by the senior vice president of the respective division.

The Role of Feedback in Driving Service Innovation

It is important to note that one key driver behind SIA's distributed innovation competence is the emphasis given to customer feedback. To encourage feedback from customers, both internal and external, SIA takes both compliments and complaints seriously. Mr Sim elaborates, "There is a vice president with responsibility for compliments and complaints, and every letter received must be acknowledged, investigated and followed up, even letters of compliment." In addition to analyzing customer complaints, compliments and suggestions, SIA collects close to 12,000 completed questionnaires a month on all its routes and travel classes in order to reliably understand the strengths and weaknesses system-wide, by geographic region, by station, by route and by travel class. The analysis can be narrowed down to very small units to nail any weaknesses in its service delivery system as well as to understand its strengths better.

Through its integrated customer feedback system, SIA gathers a large volume of feedback from its customers. However, a large proportion of customer feedback is given verbally to its front-line staff, especially cabin crew. As Mr Yap explains, "We even take verbal reports very seriously. In order for someone to sit down and write, he or she has to be either very happy or very angry. But there are always lots of little, less serious things that people don't bother to write down. If a customer mentions to a member of the crew that a meal is a little too salty, the crew member will pass on the comment to the manager. The manager will contact our food and beverage manager, who in turn will inform the caterer. So if you don't listen to the crew, you'd have let an opportunity pass, which is crazy!" Therefore, SIA's feedback system is at the same time geared to gathering and processing feedback from its employees, especially cabin crew, and also ground staff and back-office employees.

In addition, SIA listens attentively to its overseas staff, recognizing the importance of local country- and culture-specific knowledge, especially to a global firm with customers from all over the world. Its elaborate feedback mechanisms help it to not only hear its customers, but also understand them better. Mr Yap stresses, "The front-line staff are very important because they are in close contact with customers. So for every flight that the airline operates, it listens closely to the crew, who in turn know that management takes their feedback very seriously. If the company does not respond to their feedback, they would be disheartened."

Careful listening and understanding customers is difficult. Mr Sim elaborates, "Sometimes, passengers can't tell you what they will need; they cannot anticipate it. We have to do this for them. Anticipating needs they don't realize they have! For example, we noticed the changing tastes of passengers. They were becoming more health conscious when it comes to food, so we made the food lighter and more nutritious. We study data and observe customers in order to understand them really well, so that we can anticipate their needs." The introduction of a flight-alert service illustrates the importance of anticipating customers' needs, as Mr Yap explains, "We developed our mobile phone services largely because we believed that there would be a demand. Some people were sceptical. We were the first to introduce the alert service, which sends out a short text message

via SMS informing the customer of flight arrivals and delays."
There was also scepticism when SIA launched an inflight
e-mail service (Figure 4–6): "Some people said that the aircraft

Figure 4–6
More on-board options to meet the needs of different
travellers while they are in the air

Source: Courtesy of Singapore Airlines

was about the only sanctuary where they could get away from their work and their boss. They didn't want all that connectivity! However, when we studied the initial feedback, our customers really appreciated it. So we provided that facility. If you don't want it, you don't have to use it. But I think business people will enjoy the flight more if they have cleared their e-mail! Often, business people feel very stressed in the last hours before they leave the office, so with this service we can say to them, 'Relax, you don't have to be so frantic. You can take your time on board to deal with those last-minute problems.' We study the trends and try to be proactive."

All feedback is recorded and transferred to the relevant departments for immediate action, as well as to a central unit that tabulates, analyses, maps the trend, and then reports the aggregate result back to the departments. As a result, individual departments have plenty of first-hand opportunities to introduce small yet significant improvements continually. Besides providing useful insights for individual departments and reinforcing SIA's distributed innovation competence, the comments and feedback also help the product innovation department to identify opportunities to surprise and delight its customers.

SIA, a Master of Innovation

SIA has shown in the past 30 years and more that it can deliver sustained cost-effective service excellence enabled at least partially through its innovation capabilities. It employs a unique approach to new-service development that seamlessly combines hard, structured, rigorous and centralized innovation, led mainly by the product innovation department, with soft, emergent and distributed innovation led by different functional departments. These capabilities are complemented by an integrated customer and front-line staff feedback system that provides valuable insights for both the product innovation department and the functional departments, and together they reinforce SIA's innovation competence.

NOTE

This chapter is partly based on interviews with SIA executives conducted in 2001–2005. Because of the time lapse, the designations of some interviewees have changed. The following list of interviewees (in alphabetical order) shows the title of the individuals at the time of the interview and, in parentheses, their present designation if different:

- Choo Poh Leong, Senior Manager, Cabin Crew Performance (now Senior Manager, Crew Services)
- Timothy Chua, Project Manager, New Service Development (now Senior Manager, Inflight Services (Projects))
- Dr Goh Ban Eng, Senior Manager, Cabin Crew Training (now Senior Manager, Human Resource Development)
- Lam Seet Mui, Senior Manager for Human Resource Development (now Senior Manager, Cabin Crew Training)
- Lim Suu Kuan, Commercial Training Manager
- Sim Kay Wee, then Senior Vice President, Cabin Crew (Mr Sim left SIA since the interviews were conducted)
- Toh Giam Ming, Senior Manager, Crew Performance
- Betty Wong, Senior Manager, Cabin Crew Service Development (now Acting Vice President, Inflight Services)
- Yap Kim Wah, Senior Vice President, Product and Service
- Dr Yeoh Teng Kwong, then Senior Manager, Product Innovation (Dr Yeoh left SIA since the interviews were conducted)

5

Managing People Effectively to Deliver Sustained Service Excellence

Behind most of today's successful service organizations stands a firm commitment to effective management of human resources, including recruitment, selection, training, motivation and retention of employees.[1] Leading service firms are often characterized by a distinctive culture, strong service leadership and role modelling by top management. It is probably harder for competitors to duplicate high-performance human assets than any other corporate resource. In addition, service staff can be crucially important for a firm's competitive positioning because of the characteristics of the front line:

- **It is a core part of the product.** As soon as front-line staff are involved in a service process, they tend to be the most visible element of the service, as they are the people delivering the service and hence significantly determining service quality. In the case of SIA, its front-line staff – the Singapore Girls – have become synonymous with SIA and the personification of quality service.[2] They are one of the airline industry's most instantly recognizable figures, giving SIA a key competitive advantage as no other airline has managed to 'brand' and promote its cabin crew as successfully.

- **It is the service firm.** Front-line staff represent the service firm and, from a customer's perspective, is the firm. Front-line staff at SIA are empowered to make appropriate decisions to customize service delivery and take corrective actions instantaneously during service recovery.

- **It is the brand.** Front-line staff and service are often a core part of the brand. It is the staff who determine whether the brand promise gets delivered or not. Understanding that, SIA places heavy emphasis on all aspects of the selection, training and motivation of its staff in general, and its front line in particular.

In this chapter, we will focus on the people side of SIA's sustained service excellence. Specifically, we will discuss the following:

- The five key elements behind SIA's effective human resource management strategy and how each of the five elements reinforces SIA's service excellence strategy.
- The problems posed by strained industrial relations in SIA and the challenges it faces in restoring relations. The challenges mostly result from recent crises in the aviation industry (the 11 September terror attacks and SARS) and the recent entry of a number of budget carriers into Asia.

The Five Key Elements of SIA's Human Resource Management Strategy

From the interviews with SIA's senior management, we deduce that there are five interrelated and mutually supportive elements behind SIA's effective human resource management strategy. Together with the leadership and role modelling of its top management, these five elements are an important part of the explanation of how SIA has managed to consistently deliver cost-effective service excellence for over three decades through the effective and strategic management of one of its greatest assets – which is its human resources.

As shown in Figure 5–1, these five elements are stringent selection and recruitment of people, extensive training and retraining of employees, formation of successful service delivery teams, empowerment of front-line staff, and motivation of employees. These elements are emphasized in successful human resource management, especially in the field of strategic human resource management, and they have been shown to lead to higher company performance.[3] However, many service firms have not been able to implement them successfully. Now let us take a closer look at how the five elements work and complement each other at SIA.

Figure 5–1
The five elements behind SIA's effective
human resource management strategy

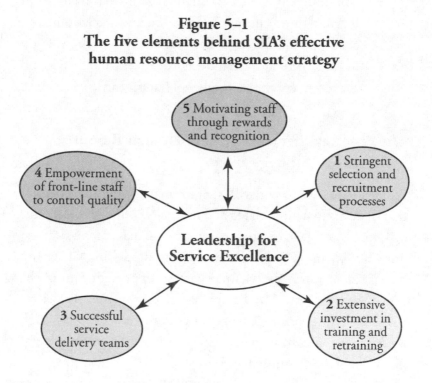

Stringent selection and recruitment processes

As Jim Collins said, "The old adage 'People are the most important asset' is wrong. The right people are your most important asset." We would like to add to this: "… and the wrong people are a liability." Getting it right starts with hiring the right people. To support its service excellence strategy, SIA adopts a rigorous system and process for staff selection and recruitment.

Cabin crew applicants, who must be under 26 years of age, are initially assessed on both academic qualifications and physical attributes. If they meet the baseline requirements for these qualities, they then go through an extensive recruitment process that involves three rounds of interviews, a uniform check, a water confidence test, a psychometric test and a tea party. Out of 16,000 applications received annually, around 500 to 600 new cabin crew members are hired to cover turnover rates of around 10%, which include both voluntary and directed attrition. When new cabin crew staff start flying, they are carefully monitored for the first six months through a monthly report by the inflight supervisor. At the end of the probationary period, around 75% of them are confirmed for an initial five-year contract, around 20% have their probation extended, and around 5% leave.

Because of the special social status and glamour associated with SIA's cabin crew (see Figure 5–2), many educated young women and men from all over Asia apply every year to join the ranks of SIA. And because of SIA's reputation as a service leader in the airline industry and as a company that develops its staff in an extensive and holistic manner, it can have its pick of talented young people. Many job seekers in Asia, especially school leavers and university graduates, see SIA as a desirable company to work for, often opening the door to more lucrative jobs in other companies.

Figure 5–2
The Singapore Girl, the leading figure of SIA's
international marketing and advertising campaigns since
the airline's establishment in 1972

Courtesy of Singapore Airlines.

What does SIA look for in applicants? According to Choo
Poh Leong, Senior Manager (Crew Services), SIA looks for cabin
crew applicants "who have that empathy with people. We try to
see whether the person is cheerful, friendly, humble, because we

don't want the person to fly and then take on a passenger and give him or her a bad time on board the plane." Shortlisted applicants go through various rounds of interviews. The first one is a group interview where the interviewers assess the applicants' overall looks and personality and their command of English. Typically, applicants are asked to introduce themselves and talk about themselves, and then to read a passage for the interviewers to assess their standard of English. This interview is not in-depth. If successful in the initial round, the applicant moves on to a one-on-one interview during which the interviewer will ask in-depth questions to assess whether the applicant has the core values and competencies SIA desires in its cabin crew. Successful applicants from this second round, then go through a psychometric test, which is conducted to confirm the results of the earlier interviews.

Following that, the applicants proceed to what SIA calls a uniform check, when they will put on the sarong kebaya, SIA's uniform for female cabin crew. At this stage, the mostly female interviewers will assess how an applicant looks in the sarong kebaya in terms of posture, gait and general looks. Successful candidates will then go through a water confidence test at SIA's training pool in its flight safety wing. Applicants, wearing a life jacket, are required to jump from a height of three metres into the pool. Because successful applicants will later, as part of their training, have to learn how to help passengers during an emergency evacuation on water, they cannot have a fear of water or heights.

The next interview is what SIA calls the management round. Here, the senior vice president (Cabin Crew) and one of the senior staff of cabin crew services interview all the applicants who have been shortlisted after the earlier rounds. This two-on-one interview is again in-depth in order to ensure that the right applicants are picked. After this round, the final assessment is made. The last step after this assessment is a tea party for the successful applicants. According to Mr Choo, "We mix with them, we talk to them, to reconfirm for us. In case in the two-to-one round we have certain doubts about you, we'd like to see you in a different setting; or we may have made certain judgement on you, we'd like to reconfirm in that management tea party round. So once you get through that, then you are selected."

This rigorous selection process ensures with reasonable certainty that SIA hires the cabin crew it desires and eliminates less suitable candidates. The result is that only some 3% to 4% of the applicants are hired.

Extensive investment in training and retraining

When a firm has good people in the first place, investment in training and retraining can then yield outstanding results. Service champions show a strong commitment to training in terms of resources and action. As Schneider and Bowen put it, "The combination of attracting a diverse and competent applicant pool, utilizing effective techniques for hiring the most appropriate people from that pool, and then training the heck out of them would be gangbusters in any market."[4]

Our interviews with SIA's senior management clearly reveal that the airline places considerable emphasis on training, so much so that training is one of its focal points in its human resource and service excellence strategy. According to Ms Lam Seet Mui, Senior Manager for Human Resource Development, "SIA invests huge amounts of money in infrastructure and technology, but, ultimately, you need people to drive it. At SIA, we believe that people actually do make a difference, so the company has in place a very comprehensive and holistic approach to developing our human resources. Essentially, we do two types of training, namely functional training and general management-type training."

Although training is regularly highlighted as a key component in the cycle of success for service firms,[5] no other airline appears to put as much emphasis as SIA on the training of its front-line staff. For example, a newly recruited batch of cabin crew are required to go through an intensive four-month training course which is considered to be the longest and most comprehensive in the airline industry.[6] In addition, flight crew are also required to go through 29 months of comprehensive 'on-line training' before being promoted to first officer[7] (Figure 5–3).

The aim of SIA's training is to provide gracious service reflecting warmth and friendliness while maintaining an image of authority and confidence in the passengers' minds. Each month, thousands of prospective cabin crew employees apply for the airline's rigorous and holistic course that encompasses not only safety and functional training but also beauty tips, gourmet food and fine wine appreciation, and the art of conversation.[8] According to Mr Choo, "During the four months' training, they go through various courses. Typically, they have

Figure 5–3
SIA pilots are required to complete 29 months of
comprehensive training before they are allowed to
take off and land a plane

Courtesy of Singapore Airlines.

to go through modules like the SIA Way, where they are taught what is expected from them in SIA, passenger handling skills, food and beverage skills, service attributes and grooming. We pay a lot of attention to grooming and deportment. They also attend various safety training courses, which are conducted by our flight safety department. They cover first aid, safety equipment and procedures, evacuation procedures, and handling of unruly passengers. So it's quite a comprehensive training course. When they pass the course, then they can fly. They are put on probation for six months. But training doesn't stop after that; there's continuous training. So even crew members who are flying have to come back for further training."

Because of its reputation for service excellence, SIA's customers tend to have very high expectations and can be very demanding, which can put considerable pressure on its front-line staff. According to Ms Lim Suu Kuan, Commercial Training Manager, the motto of SIA is this: If SIA can't do it for you, no other airline can. The challenge is to help the staff deal with difficult situations and take the brickbats. The company helps its staff deal with the emotional turmoil of having to satisfy and even please very demanding customers without feeling that they are being taken advantage of.

According to former CEO Dr Cheong Choong Kong, "To the company, training is forever and no one is too young to be trained, nor too old." Yap Kim Wah, Senior Vice President (Product and Service) adds, "We believe that there is no moment, regardless of how senior a staff is, when you cannot learn something. So all of us, senior vice presidents included, are sent for training regularly. We all have a training path. You can always pick up something. If you have completed quite a number of programmes, then you go for sabbatical. You go and learn a language, do something new and refresh yourself." Such continuous training and retraining has been vital to SIA in sustaining service excellence; it helps staff to have an open mindset, to accept change and development, and to deliver the new services that SIA introduces regularly (Figure 5–4).

There are seven training schools in the SIA Group dedicated to delivering training in each of the seven core functional areas: cabin crew, flight operations, commercial training, information

Figure 5–4
Delivering warm, friendly and competent service:
The result of extensive training that equips
front-line staff with the required skills and attitude

Courtesy of Singapore Airlines.

technology, security, airport services training, and engineering. General management training is offered by the SIA Management Development Centre (MDC), which is under the purview of the human resources division. It provides executive and leadership programmes for staff from all sections of the company with the aim of generating effective administrators as well as visionary managers. This training is centralized so that the engineers get to meet the computer experts and the marketing people and so on. This purposeful mixing of its staff enhances mutual understanding and inculcates a more integrated and holistic view (and way of management) by all divisions. MDC's programmes are divided into three broad areas: (1) management development programmes focusing on the changing priorities and skills required at various levels of the managerial hierarchy; (2) management skills development programmes which are functional or skills related, ranging from the art of negotiation to the learning of other cultures; (3) self-development programmes in areas such as social etiquette.[9]

SIA trains about 9,000 people a year and is well known for its dynamic and committed approach to training. According to Ms Lam, "About 70% of SIA's courses are done in-house, and one of SIA's recent service excellence initiative, called Transforming Customer Service (TCS), involves staff in five key operational areas: cabin crew, engineering, ground services, flight operations, and sales support. To ensure that the TCS culture is promoted company-wide, it is also embedded into all management training. MDC has put together a two-day management training programme entitled TCS Operational Areas Strategy Implementing Synergy (OASIS). The programme also aims at building team spirit among our staff in key operational areas so that together we will make the whole journey as pleasant and seamless as possible for our passengers. One has to realize that it is not just the ticketing or reservations people and the cabin crew who come into contact with our passengers. The pilots, station managers and station engineers have a role in customer service as well, because from time to time they do come into contact with passengers. But TCS is not just about people. In TCS, there is the 40-30-30 rule, which is a holistic approach to people, processes (or procedures) and products. SIA focuses 40% of the resources on training and invigorating our people, 30% on reviewing processes and procedures, and 30% on creating new product and service ideas." The focus is thus on the totality rather than just one aspect of customer service, and this enables the airline to deliver a service that is excellent in all aspects.

One of the main forces behind the success of SIA's training and retraining programmes is its leadership, as well as the relationship management builds with staff. As Timothy Chua, Project Manager (New Service Development) puts it, "I see myself first as a coach and second as a team player." Instead of positioning themselves as managers or superiors, SIA's management often view themselves as mentors and coaches, guiding and imparting knowledge and experience to new recruits and new department members.

To ensure that its management understands the big picture, SIA trains all management staff through job rotation. Managers are rotated to other departments every few years. This strategy produces a number of benefits. It allows managers to acquire an understanding of the workings of more sections of the organization than they would otherwise. It also promotes a corporate outlook, reduces interdepartmental disputes, and creates an appetite for change and innovation as people constantly bring fresh perspectives and new ideas to their new positions.

Building high-performance service delivery teams

The nature of many types of services requires people to work in teams, often across functions, in order to deliver seamless customer service. Effective teams facilitate communication and knowledge sharing among team members, thus enabling the members to understand and learn from each other.

In view of the importance of teamwork in the delivery of service excellence, SIA endeavours to create esprit de corps among its cabin crew. Its approach to developing teamwork among its diverse group of cabin crew staff is the team concept, which involves dividing the 6,600 crew members into small units with a team leader in charge of about 13 people. Members of the team are rostered to fly together as much as possible. Flying together as a unit allows them to build camaraderie and get to know each other. The team leader also gets to know each member's strengths and weaknesses well and becomes their mentor and counsel, someone to whom they can turn to if they need help or advice. In addition, there are 'check trainers' who oversee 12 or 13 teams and fly with them whenever possible, not only to inspect their performance but also to help the teams develop.

According to Sim Kay Wee, Senior Vice President (Cabin Crew), "The interaction within each of the teams is very strong. As a result, when team leaders do staff appraisal, they really know the staff. You would be amazed how meticulous and detailed each staff record is, even though there are 6,600 of them. We can pinpoint any staff's strengths and weaknesses easily. So, in this way, we have good control; and through this, we can ensure that the crew delivers the promise. If there are problems, we will know about them and we can send them for retraining. Those who are good will be selected for promotion."

According to Toh Giam Ming, Senior Manager (Crew Performance), "What is good about the team concept is that, despite the huge number of crew members, people can relate to a team and have a sense of belonging: 'This is my team.' They are put together for one to two years and are rostered together for about 60% to 70% of the time, so they do fly together quite a fair bit. So, especially for the new people, I think they find that they have less problem adjusting to the flying career, no matter what their background is. Because once you get familiar with the team, there is support and guidance on how to do things." Mr Choo adds, "The individual, you see, is not a digit or a staff number. If you don't have team flying, with 6,000-odd people it can be difficult for you to really know a particular person."

SIA also has a lot of seemingly unrelated activities in the cabin crew division. For example, there is the performing arts circle made up of talented employees with an interest in the arts. During the biennial cabin crew gala dinner in

2004, SIA employees raised over half a million dollars for charity.[10] In addition to the performing arts circle, there are also a gourmet circle, language circles (such as a German and French speaking group) and even sports circles (such as football and tennis teams). The company believes that these activities encourage camaraderie and teamwork (Figure 5–5).

Figure 5–5
SIA crew members contributing to charity
while fostering team spirit

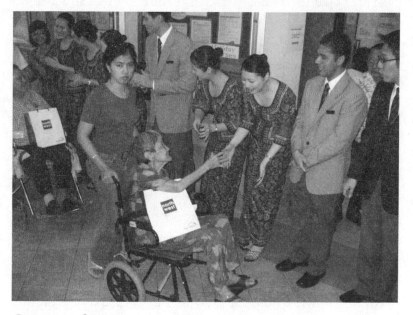

Courtesy of Singapore Airlines.

Empowerment of front-line staff to control quality

Virtually all outstanding service firms have legendary stories of employees who recovered failed service transactions, walked the extra mile to make a customer's day, or averted some kind of disaster for a client. Mr Toh shares such a story: "This particular passenger was a wheelchair-bound lady in her eighties, was very ill, suffering from arthritis. She was travelling from Singapore to Brisbane. What happened was that a stewardess found her gasping for air owing to crippling pain. The stewardess used her personal hot-water bottle as a warm compress to relieve the passenger's pain and knelt to massage the lady's legs and feet for 45 minutes. By that time, the lady's feet were actually swollen. The stewardess offered her a new pair of flight support stockings without asking her to pay for them. She basically took care of the old lady throughout the trip, seven to eight hours. When the old lady got back to Brisbane, her son called the hotel in which the crew were staying to try and trace this stewardess to thank her personally. He then followed up with a letter to us. I don't know if training contributes to it, or if it is personal. I mean, you don't find people who'd do this purely as a result of training, I think. We find the right people, give them the right support, give them the right training, and with the right support people will do this kind of thing."

Such thoughtful actions are part of the culture at SIA. According to Mr Choo, the crew members "are very proud to be part of the SIA team, very proud of the tradition and very proud that SIA is held up as a company that gives excellent care to customers. So they want to live up to that."

Employees have to feel empowered to engage in such discretionary efforts. Employees making decisions on their own have become increasingly important, especially in service firms, because front-line staff frequently have to handle customers on their own, and it tends to be difficult and also unproductive for managers to constantly monitor their actions closely.[11] However, one of the biggest issues many service organizations face when it comes to empowerment is that there is a lot of talk about empowerment but no concrete action. According to SIA's senior management, staff must have a clear idea of the limits of their authority, and it is the responsibility of management to articulate and make it clear what they mean by empowerment. For example, whereas the usual baggage allowance is 10 kilograms, SIA front-line staff are empowered to raise it to 25, 30 or even 50 kilograms, as long as they feel that it is a right decision. However, such a decision by a front line staff must be recorded and justified.

According to Mr Yap, as guidelines for implementing empowerment, staff should be given the authority of the people two levels up: "If you are a clerk, you should know what your officer and your senior officer can do. If these two officers are not around, you can make decisions up to the limits of their authority."

Empowerment of the front line is especially important during service recovery processes. As noted by Timothy Chua, "We strive for instantaneous service recovery. I think that is one of SIA's biggest differentiators. When something goes wrong, we react quickly; and I believe we generally do it in a very fair way."

Motivating through rewards and recognition

Once a firm has hired the right people, trained them well, empowered them and organized them in effective service delivery teams, how can it ensure that they will deliver service excellence? Staff performance is a function of ability and motivation. Reward systems are the key to motivation, and service staff must get the message that they will be recognized and rewarded for providing quality service. Motivating and rewarding strong service performers is also one of the most effective ways of retaining them.

Understanding that many service businesses fail because they do not utilize the full range of available rewards effectively, SIA offers various forms of rewards, including interesting and varied job content, symbolic forms of recognition and performance-based share options. It recently introduced equity-linked incentives for staff and linked more variable components of pay to individual staff contribution as well as to the company's financial performance.[12] Another source of motivation comes in the form of the international accolades for excellence that the airline has received over the years, which include several 'best airline', 'best cabin crew service' and 'Asia's most admired company' awards.

Additionally, the company makes use of communication to further spur its employees to deliver quality service. Company-wide meetings and briefings are held regularly to keep staff informed of the latest developments. Corporate newsletters and circulars help promote information sharing. Interaction between staff and management is encouraged through regular staff meetings. As Ms Lim notes, "It's about communication. For example, if we add a new service at check-in, we will talk to the people involved before, during and after implementation. We will discuss the importance and the value of it, and make sure everyone is aware of what we are doing and why. It helps to give staff pride in what they do."

Communication is also important in recognizing service excellence. Newsletters are used to share and recognize good service. Staff who go the extra mile are recognized through the annual Deputy Chairman's Award. Mr Sim stresses the importance of recognition, "We know that a pat on the back, a good ceremony, photographs and write-ups in the newsletters can be more motivating than mere financial rewards, hence we put in a lot of effort to ensure that heros and heroines are recognized for their commitment and dedication." SIA's performance management system is quite sophisticated and comprehensive. An outline of the cabin crew assessment system is given in the Appendix at the end of this chapter.

All in all, what makes SIA cabin crew so special that other carriers try to imitate it? Mr Choo says, "Here, there are some intangibles. I think what makes it special is a combination of many things. First, you've got to ensure that you find the right people for the job, and after that training matters a great deal: the way you nurture them, the way you monitor them and the way you reward them. The recognition you give need not necessarily be money. I think another very important ingredient is the overall culture of cabin crew, the fact that you have people who really are very proud of the tradition. And I think a lot of our senior people – and it rubs off on the junior crew – take pride in the fact that they helped build up the airline; they are very proud of it and they want to ensure that it remains that way." Mr Toh adds, "Among other contributing factors is a deeply ingrained service culture not just among the cabin crew but also in the whole company. I think it goes back to 35 years ago when the airline was set up. A very, very strong service culture throughout the whole organization, very strong commitment from top management. We take every complaint seriously. We respond to every complaint. We try to learn from the feedback; it's a never-ending process."

Managing Labour Relations

The cost-cutting measures necessitated by the company's first ever quarterly loss of S$312 million in the quarter ending July 2003 caused mainly by the SARS outbreak, and the increased competition brought by the entry of a multitude of low-cost carriers across Asia, have created strains within SIA. On 19 June 2003, CEO Chew Choon Seng announced the retrenchment of 414 Singapore-based employees (1.5% of the company's staff), comprising office staff, airport workers and engineering personnel. The retrenchment exercise was initiated as a last measure in response to the difficult operating environment, following earlier moves towards stringent cost management that included deferring discretionary spending, freezing recruitment, cutting management's pay by up to 27.5% and introducing compulsory no-pay leave for cabin crew.[13] Mr Chew announced that, "We have always said that we would consider retrenchment as a measure of last resort.

I am sad to say that we are now at that point. It is unfortunate, but there is no alternative if we are to ensure that the company survives this downturn and position ourselves to compete effectively in the marketplace of the future."

In addition to retrenchments, staff were asked to accept pay cuts and take unpaid leave. What followed was a public debate of labour–management positions in the pages of the local daily *Straits Times*. A survey of three of the four SIA unions showed lower staff morale and a perceived change in the family atmosphere, for which the carrier was known, to one of accountability in which workers feared losing their jobs.[14] Tension between pilots and the airline escalated after pay cuts were implemented in June 2003, and the situation worsened when the cuts were maintained after SIA posted a profit of S$306 million in the following quarter. Leaders of three unions – the SIA Staff Union, the Singapore Airport Terminal Services Workers Union and the SIA Engineering Company Engineers and Executives Union – were asked to provide feedback on SIA's labour–management relations. The feedback cited several areas that needed to be addressed.[15] Recognizing the tensions raised by the cost-cutting measures, the airline is trying to restore morale. Managerial and supervisory staff have been advised to be more sensitive to the needs of their staff, and top management has been receiving regular feedback to keep apprised of the situation on the ground.

It will be a challenging balancing act to further raise SIA's already high labour productivity while at the same time retaining and refining its hitherto highly successful human resource management. The recent difficult conditions caused by the outbreak of SARS, the intensifying competitive environment for full-service carriers, and the influx of budget carriers have challenged the consistent profitability of the airline. While SIA's rapid response to the crises was impressive, the stringent cost-cutting measures that were required to cope with these challenges inevitably affected morale and have the potential to undermine the company's service-oriented culture, despite efforts to assist retrenched staff, such as training programmes and workshops that included courses on managing emotions, financial planning and career guidance.[16]

In Conclusion

For over three decades, SIA has managed to achieve what many others in the aviation industry can only dream of: cost-effective service excellence that is reinforced by effective human resource management and a positive company culture and image. In this chapter, we discussed the role of SIA's leadership and the five key elements constituting SIA's human resource management strategy (i.e., stringent selection and hiring of people, followed by extensive training and retraining, formation of successful service delivery teams, empowerment of the front line, and motivating staff), which have helped SIA to build and sustain service excellence at levels consistently above the competition over three decades. The recent crises and the emergence of budget carriers require SIA to sustain its focus on achieving cost-effective service excellence and, if necessary, reexamine some aspects of its recipe for success.

Appendix: Cabin Crew Performance Management

1. How is the cabin crew area structured and how does this influence the performance management system?

    SIA's crew is formed into 36 groups known as wards, each headed by a ward leader who monitors the performance of the crew. The ward leader, in turn, reports to a cabin crew executive. Each executive is in charge of six ward leaders and also oversees other aspects of crew administration/management such as communication and welfare.

2. Describe the performance management tool/process that you use to monitor your cabin crew?

    The performance of a crew is measured through on-board assessments (OBAs) carried out by a more senior crew member on the same flight. The elements assessed are as follows:

    (a) *Image*: grooming and uniform turnout
    (b) *Service orientation*: crew's interaction and passenger handling capabilities
    (c) *Product knowledge and job skills*: performance in the various bar and meal services and familiarity with procedures as well as job and product knowledge
    (d) *Safety and security*: knowledge of and adherence to safety and security procedures
    (e) *Work relationship*: general attitude and teamwork/ team spirit

(f) *People management skills*: supervisory and people management skills, development of junior crew, ability to plan and coordinate the various services

(g) *Pre-flight session*: effectiveness of the pre-flight briefing

(Sections f and g are only applicable to the crew in-charge.)

3. How frequently is the assessment conducted?

    The frequency varies from rank to rank, and performance is tracked over a financial year.

    (a) *New crew on probation*: six OBAs during the six-month probation period, together with a closed assessment that evaluates the crew member's attitude, interest towards the job and bias or apprehension towards certain passengers

    (b) *Flight steward/stewardess*: minimum four assessments per year

    (c) *Supervisory crew*: three to four times per year

    (d) *Crew in-charge*: twice per year

4. What level of feedback is given to the individual, at the time of assessment and cumulatively (i.e., quarterly, annually, etc.)? How do you manage a good quality of interaction during the feedback rather than just making sure the meeting happens?

    The OBA is an open appraisal whereby the appraiser discusses the strengths and weaknesses with the appraisee. The appraisee will review and endorse the OBA. All returned

OBAs are scanned and flagged for the ward leader's attention if the scores fall outside our predetermined thresholds. If necessary, the ward leader will go on the appraisees' flight to check the crew out personally. The ward leader can (and often does) call in the crew for a discussion at any time if deemed necessary. Concerted effort is made for the ward leader to fly with each crew in his (or her) charge at least once a year, during which he will review and discuss the records of the crew. In addition, the ward leader is required to carry out an annual assessment of all crew members in his ward before finalizing the annual appraisal score. The annual appraisal is weighted as follows:

Element	Weightage (%)
On-board assessment	60
Discipline	15
Attendance record	10
Passenger feedback	10
Ward leader assessment	5

5. What degree of alignment is there between the company values and the areas assessed?

The company's core values are embedded in the elements assessed in the OBAs, such as service orientation and product knowledge (pursuit of excellence), safety and security (safety), and work relationship and people management (teamwork).

6. How are assessors trained and what level of ongoing training occurs to ensure rater consistency?

All crew members promoted to the supervisory rank have to attend a one-day appraisal workshop where they are taught the basics of assessment and coached on the use of the OBA form. There is also an ongoing process to review all OBAs that have been improperly done and to pick out appraisers who habitually give extreme ratings for follow-up by ward leaders.

NOTES

The conceptual underpinning of this chapter and many of the management theories referred to were taken from Christopher H. Lovelock and Jochen Wirtz, *Services Marketing: People, Technology, Strategy*, 5th ed., Upper Saddle River, NJ: Prentice Hall, 2004. Much of the material on SIA discussed in this chapter is based on interviews conducted in 2001–2005 with the SIA executives whose names appear in the endnote of Chapter 4.

1   Benjamin Schneider and David E. Bowen, *Winning the Service Game*, Boston, MA: Harvard Business School Press, 1995, p. 131.
2   Daniel Chan, 'Beyond Singapore Girl: Brand and product/service differentiation strategies in the new millennium', *Journal of Management Development*, 19, no. 6 (2000): 515–42.
3   M. A. Huselid, S. E. Jackson and R. S. Schuler, 'Technical and strategic human resource management effectiveness as determinants of firm performance', *Academy of Management Journal*, 40 (1997): 171–88.
4   See note 1.
5   Leonard Schlesinger and James L. Heskett, 'Breaking the cycle of failure in service', *Sloan Management Review*, 31 (Spring 1991): 17–28.
6   Swapna G. Kingi and S. Dutta, *Customer Service at Singapore Airlines*, Hyderabad, India: ICFAI Centre for Management Research, 2003.
7   'Crew training', SIA press release, January 2005.
8   Daniel Chan, 'The story of Singapore Airlines and the Singapore Girl', *Journal of Management Development*, 19, no. 6 (2000): 456–72.

9   'Human resources', SIA press release, January 2005.

10   'Singapore Airlines cabin crew collect over half a million dollars for local charity', 25 September 2004, *www.singaporeair.com/saa/app/ saa?dynamic=PressReleases/NE_4904.html.*

11   Dana Yagil, 'The relationship of customer satisfaction and service workers' perceived control: Examination of three models', *International Journal of Service Industry Management*, 13, no. 4 (2002): 382–98.

12   'Labour-management relations in SIA', 1 March 2004, *www.singaporeair. com/saa/app/saa?dynamic=PressReleases/NTE_1504.html.*

13   'SIA Group to retrench 414 staff', 19 June 2003, *www.singaporeair. com/saa/app/saa?dynamic=PressReleases/NTE_2603.html.*

14   Michael Mecham, 'Adapt or die', *Aviation Week and Space Technology*, 1 March 2004.

15   See note 12.

16   See note 13.

FOR THE FIRST TIME IN HISTORY, YOU CAN FLY NON-STOP BETWEEN SINGAPORE AND LOS ANGELES.

SINGAPORE AIRLINES' NEW A345LeaderShip IS MAKING THE WORLD A SMALLER PLACE.

Singapore Airlines can now fly you half way round the world without stopping, with daily services between Singapore and Los Angeles. And soon, between Singapore and New York. Designed with the executive traveller in mind, our A345LeaderShip introduces a new long-haul travel experience. Enjoy an even more luxurious Raffles Class, and our acclaimed SpaceBed, the biggest business class bed in the sky. Our entirely new Executive Economy Class offers wide, roomy seats, and a cosy passenger area where you can socialise and enjoy a snack. Together with in-seat power for laptops and KrisWorld, the world's most advanced inflight entertainment system, the executive traveller can work, relax, or sleep in even greater space and comfort. All, of course, while enjoying the inflight service even other airlines talk about.

www.singaporeair.com

6

How to Win in Cutthroat Industries: Lessons from Singapore Airlines

We undertook this study to gain a deeper understanding of the factors that can help a company achieve sustainable success in extremely tough industries. Our findings are based on a detailed study of the strategy and organizational features of a company that has achieved just that. In this chapter, we outline some strategic lessons from this study that we believe can be applied to any company that wants to achieve competitive differentiation. We do not aim to provide the solution but rather to suggest useful strategic principles and to help executives ask the right questions which is in our mind the only approach to effective strategic thinking.

The chapter begins by reminding us why it is so hard to be successful in the airline industry. It then proceeds with lessons relating to the need to be clear about the company's generic strategy (or a combination of generic strategies), the need to have high levels of strategic alignment, the importance of nurturing and investing in capabilities and core competencies that support the strategy, and the need to understand and foster strategic innovation. We end by suggesting that, even though SIA has definitely gained from being located in a supportive institutional context, this is far from a comprehensive explanation of its success. Rather, its success can ultimately be traced to robust strategies, seamless execution, and continuous vigilance and realignment.

Why Is It So Hard to Be Successful in the Airline Industry?

We have discussed the airline industry in detail in Chapter 1. It is worth briefly reminding ourselves, however, of the main characteristics of this industry and why it is so hard to be successful in it. In the last 25 years, global demand for air travel has been growing at a reasonably healthy pace of just over 5% per annum in terms of revenue passenger-kilometres and just below 4% per annum in passenger numbers (compared with a growth of around 3.3% for the world's gross domestic product).

However, revenues in real dollars have been growing at a lower rate of 2.8% per annum, indicating a squeeze in ticket prices and, barring efficiency improvement, a consequent squeeze in margins. These pricing pressures reflect the effects of an increase in supply (from new entrants and incumbents) brought about by deregulation in an industry suffering from significant overcapacity, where on average one-third of airplane seats are empty. The bargaining power of buyers,[1] in addition, has been increasing because technological advances have led to high price transparency and more choices for customers, who have low switching costs, through buying on the Internet. These factors have encouraged commoditization of air travel, where, in the absence of any significant differentiation, many buyers make purchasing decisions based on price.

The rivalry among established firms has risen substantially, often degenerating into vicious price wars that ultimately make the whole industry worse off in terms of returns. High exit barriers, the entry of low-cost rivals, overcapacity and the maturity of the industry in most parts of the world only serve to raise rivalry to unsustainable levels. Airline alliances, offering the option of more destinations with less hassle to passengers, often achieve little in terms of granting competitive differentiation to incumbents, since every major competitor belongs to such an alliance. To make things worse, in many cases structural inertia due to regulatory or nationalist constraints does not allow industry consolidation that could raise efficiency. All these factors can shed light on the abysmal performance of the airline industry in terms of return on investment. Even among low-cost carriers, only a handful are consistently profitable (Ryanair, EasyJet and Southwest Airlines).

As *The Economist* (October 2003) has aptly commented, "The airline business is an aberration. Distorted by decades of subsidies and international cartels, it has never earned a real rate of return on its investors' capital in its 60 years of existence." In this context, SIA not only has never made a loss on an annual basis but has delivered superior returns over the years compared with its competitors. We have aimed to understand more about SIA's exceptional performance and offer our own interpretation of its success in this book.

Selecting Generic Strategies

A first step to understanding how SIA's exceptional performance has been achieved is to look at its generic strategy. Michael Porter argues that firms have to make a clear choice between a cost leadership and a differentiation strategy, otherwise they risk being 'stuck in the middle'.[2] According to Porter, the fundamental basis of above-average performance in the long run is sustainable competitive advantage. Combining the two basic types of competitive advantage that a firm can possess – low cost or differentiation – with the scope of activities for which a firm seeks to achieve them and we have three generic strategies. Further, achieving competitive advantage requires a firm to make a choice; being 'all things to all people' is a recipe for strategic mediocrity and below-average performance, because it often means that a firm has no competitive advantage at all.

Porter accepts that there can be three possibilities where a firm can achieve both cost leadership and differentiation: (1) if competitors are stuck in the middle (i.e., they have not really achieved any of these strategies); (2) if cost is strongly affected by the market share of inter-company relationships (i.e., a company that can produce a high-quality product and at the same time has a large market share will also enjoy lower average costs); and (3) if a firm pioneers a major innovation that can simultaneously raise quality and lower costs. However, he believes that all these situations are temporary, since such advantages can be swiftly imitated by competitors, and that a firm will at some point still have to make a clear choice: "A firm should always aggressively pursue all cost reduction opportunities that do not sacrifice differentiation. A firm should also pursue all differentiation opportunities that are not costly. Beyond this point, however, a firm should be prepared to choose what its ultimate competitive advantage will be and resolve the tradeoffs accordingly."

Porter's conviction that a firm has to ultimately make a choice is based on the different and often conflicting organizational and investment requirements that a successful strategy of cost leadership or differentiation entails. A cost leader would aim to cut costs at all parts of the value chain, standardize its offerings, build a culture of leanness and minimal waste, and compete on the basis of an acceptable product offered to the mass market at low prices. Companies such as EasyJet, Suzuki and Bic would be apt examples of this strategy. A differentiator, on the other hand, would be very careful about quality at every stage of the value chain, invest in innovation and customer service, build a culture of customer and market orientation, target specific value-added market segments, and compete on the basis of superior-quality products sold at premium prices. Companies such as Rolex, BMW and Harley-Davidson are good examples of differentiators. Achieving both strategies would indeed involve incompatible organizational choices for most companies.

If we examine SIA from this angle, however, we can see elements of both these generic strategies successfully inter- twined (as elaborated in Chapters 2 and 3). Differentiation at SIA is achieved through service excellence and superior quality; premium pricing for first- and business-class travel, and even for economy class, particularly when originating a trip from Singapore; high brand equity in the caring and elegant Singapore Girl; a young fleet (5 years versus industry average of 12.5 years) enhancing the flight experience; offering the world's most advanced inflight entertainment system, KrisFlyer; having Changi Airport, arguably one of the best airports in the world, as its base; and, finally, building cultural values emphasizing constant innovation and customer orientation.

All these are surprisingly not achieved at a cost penalty, however. SIA has several cost advantages that make up for the high costs associated with providing quality: it has significantly lower labour costs than its major competitors. Its young fleet is more fuel efficient and incurs lower maintenance costs than older aircraft. Its diversification through efficient subsidiaries into related services (maintenance, catering, cargo, airport services) contributes to cost efficiency. Its effective use of technology increases efficiency (e.g., telephone, Internet and SMS check- in). And, finally, cost consciousness permeates the airline.

All these factors allow SIA to successfully combine differentiation with a low-cost strategy.[3] Indeed, both superior quality as well as high levels of efficiency have been part of the goals and objectives of SIA since its founding, which are to deliver the highest quality of customer service that is safe, reliable and economical; to generate earnings that provide sufficient resources for investment and satisfactory returns to shareholders; to adopt human resource management practices company-wide that attract, develop, motivate and retain employees who contribute to the company's objectives; and to maximize productivity and utilization of all resources.

One lesson here is that it is possible to combine elements of differentiation and low-cost strategies. Besides SIA, other companies such as Dell and Intel have achieved this integration. In each case, the precise elements that are integrated vary, but the result is the same: an unbeatable strategic combination. What is your company's generic strategy? Is it possible to integrate elements of both differentiation and low cost in your company's strategy? How can you implement this integration?

Achieving Strategic Alignment

Strategic alignment can be seen from two main perspectives: vertical or hierarchical and horizontal. In a vertical or hierarchical sense, it refers to the consistency among four elements: (1) the strategy, (2) the core competencies, (3) the organizational features or functional strategies that implement or operationalize the strategy, and (4) the external environment. In a horizontal sense, strategic alignment is the mutual reinforcement, support and consistency among organizational features, functional strategies, or elements of the value chain.

An apt example of horizontal strategic alignment is Ikea. All the elements of its value chain are mutually consistent in support of a business strategy of cost leadership. Table 6–1 compares the value chain of Ikea with that of traditional furniture manufacturers which compete with a business strategy of differentiation.

In Chapter 3, we elaborated on SIA's five organizational pillars supporting its core competence of cost-effective service excellence. Chapter 4 expanded on SIA's innovation capacity (the pillar of total innovation), and Chapter 5 on its human resource management practices (the pillar of holistic staff development). SIA's core competency in turn supports its strategy of achieving high levels of profitability and differentiation through providing excellent service, continuous innovation and high efficiency, and it is aligned with what customers value in the airline industry. In terms of horizontal alignment, the mutual reinforcement, consistency and support among SIA's operational features were illustrated through SIA's activity map in Chapter 3. We can thus see that SIA exhibits a high level of strategic alignment.

In fact, the five pillars of SIA's core competency of cost-effective service excellence correspond to key organizational features to which any organization has to pay close attention: *culture*, *people*, *structure* and process. 'Ingrained profit consciousness' is a key aspect of culture in SIA, 'holistic staff development' corresponds to the dimension of people, 'strategic synergies' correspond to the dimension of structure, and 'total

Table 6–1

Strategic alignment at Ikea versus traditional furniture makers

	Design	Parts	Assembly	Logistics	Marketing	Service
Traditional furniture makers	Independent designers	High levels of work in progress	Labour intensive	Relatively inefficient supply chain	Fragmented geographically	Full-service
	Complex, tailored designs	Handicraft, custom manufacturing	Built to order	Transport costly, bulky finished products	Expensive, high-street displays	Small-lot delivery to customer
Ikea	In-house designers	Modular, interchangeable parts	Minimal assembly by company	Computerized, efficient	Leverage on Scandinavian image	Self-service
	Simple designs	Cheaper materials, mass production	Assembly by customer	Transport modular parts	Cheap out-of-town displays	Customer's own transport for small items

innovation' and 'rigorous service design', correspond to the dimension of process. SIA's strategic alignment is portrayed in Figure 6–1.

Figure 6–1
SIA's strategic alignment between organization, capabilities and strategy

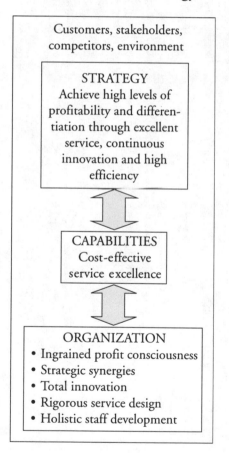

Strategic alignment is a relatively simple idea to grasp, but it is surprising how difficult it is to get right, or how many misaligned or even conflicting practices one can observe in organizations. One classic form of misalignment is "the folly of rewarding A while hoping for B".[4] We see companies rewarding employees based on individual performance yet hoping for teamwork and value sharing, or rewarding managers based purely on the firm's financial performance yet hoping that customers receive a great experience through their interaction with the company. In the academe, academics get rewarded chiefly for their research productivity (with rewards such as tenure, full professorship or a post in a world-class university), yet great teaching and earnest performance in administrative duties are also hoped for.

A second form of misalignment occurs when the organization, capabilities and strategy are aligned internally but are misaligned with external factors, the demands of the competitive environment. In the mid-1990s, many Western brewing giants rushed into the China beer market investing billions building state-of-the-art factories to produce premium beer sold under their global brands, only to painfully discover that the premium segment of the market was miniscule, consumers were fiercely loyal to their local brands, local competitors engaged in predatory price cutting, and the local administrations were not always welcoming or easy to deal with. While these global competitors had a high level of alignment internally, they were not aligned with what the market wanted or could support, nor with the institutional environment. The result was that most of them left China, unable to keep sustaining huge losses year after year, selling their state-of-the-art factories to local competitors such as Tsingtao at bargain basement prices.[5]

A third form of misalignment occurs when a company has a highly aligned model, both internally as well as with the external environment, but it does not keep in touch with external changes and does not realign when the environment changes. A firm that failed to realign and went bankrupt was Wang, once the leader in network enterprise computing. Wang failed to appreciate that the arrival of the personal computer would encroach on its market and that it would in fact be cheaper for companies to buy several personal computers for their employees rather than Wang's expensive system that tied companies to the vendor for costly regular maintenance. A company that managed to realign successfully is IBM. Realizing that hardware was gradually becoming commodified, it focused on services, adopting the motto "providing solutions for a small planet". IBM gradually reduced its investment in hardware manufacturing and increased its capabilities in services and consulting, realigning itself with market trends and refocusing on new profit pools.[6]

A final form of misalignment is the most regrettable type. It occurs when managers take actions that destroy the company's capabilities, believing that the result would be alignment with a new strategy or a new environmental imperative. When the managers of Schlitz beer, once the number 2 beer in the United States, decided to reduce costs by using cheaper ingredients for production and shortening the production cycle, competitors promptly leaked this news to the market and its market share began a free fall. Even after the company decided to reinstate the previous production processes, it could not save Schlitz; the brand image had been tarnished and the company went bankrupt. A common misalignment seen today results from the mishandling of reengineering efforts. Morale is destroyed in the process, while productivity and profitability are but only temporarily enhanced. The best swimmers jump off the sinking ship first in such cases, and the company's capability base is duly depleted. Some argue that the recent and highly contested Hewlett Packard–Compaq merger amounted to a de facto destruction of capabilities and shareholder value for HP, since the combined market value of the two companies is close to the value of HP's printer division alone.

These examples show that achieving and maintaining alignment requires clear thinking, seamless execution, discipline and constant vigilance in keeping in touch with external changes, fine-tuning and, if necessary, realigning to maintain a winning position. How aligned is your company, both vertically and horizontally? Are you keeping in touch with the market, and is there a need for realignment?

The Role of Capabilities and Core Competencies

The resource-based view of strategy, introduced to the field around 20 years ago,[7] has focused attention on internal, company-related factors, as opposed to planning prowess (the strategic planning view) or the selection of specific industry niches (the industrial analysis view), as crucial for competitive success. In the resource-based view, companies can win if they have access to resources or if they can develop certain capabilities that are valuable to customers, rare or unique, hard to imitate and hard to substitute. Capabilities make all the difference as to how a given set of resources is managed, and different organizations with broadly similar sets of resources can achieve markedly different outcomes and performance.

If we compare Kmart and Wal-Mart and look for the reasons for which Wal-Mart won the competitive battle, we can see that the differentiating capability that helped it overtake Kmart was logistics efficiency, which reduced costs by 2%–3%, a significant advantage in retailing. Wal-Mart pioneered the process of cross-docking and invested in a private satellite communications system and a dedicated truck fleet at the time when most of its competitors were outsourcing these as non-core functions. Similarly, Dell has been a market leader with good performance in personal computers, at a time when the industry is saturated and commoditized and most competitors are losing money. Dell's success can be explained by its differentiating capability of mass customization, real-time market monitoring, and high levels of efficiency at all stages of the value chain. IBM's deep pockets were not able to make up for Dell's distinctive capabilities, so it progressively exited the computer hardware market and instead focuses on service-related offerings.

All companies have resources, tangible and intangible, and all companies have various capabilities, or the ability to organize resources effectively and efficiently to realize its strategy. Capabilities are intangible, embedded in people, processes and culture; and they are much harder to copy than tangible resources, which often can be imitated successfully as long as money is available. However, few companies have capabilities that satisfy the four criteria of being valuable to customers, rare, hard to imitate and hard to substitute. These capabilities can be referred to as core competencies that lead to sustainable competitive advantage, and companies that have them are more likely to achieve superior performance than their competitors in the longer term (see Figure 6–2).

Figure 6–2
The relationship between resources, capabilities, core competencies and sustainable competitive advantage

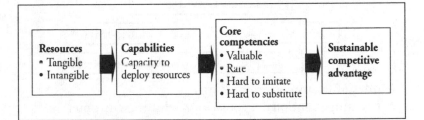

There are three main classes of capabilities: operational excellence, customer orientation, and innovation (see Figure 6–3). If we examine any world-leading company, we will see that it excels in one or more of these capabilities to such an extent that the capabilities become the company's core competencies. Capabilities are multi-dimensional, and companies can excel in different dimensions. One aspect of operational excellence is efficiency, which means achieving similar outputs at a lower cost than the company's peers (as

Figure 6–3
Examples of companies known for their
(a) operational excellence, (b) customer orientation or
(c) innovation capability

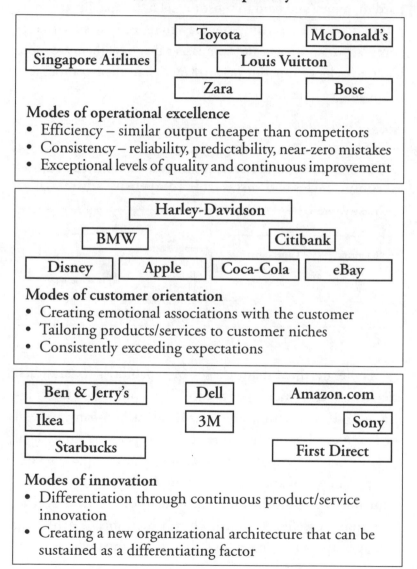

Toyota   McDonald's
Singapore Airlines   Louis Vuitton
Zara   Bose

Modes of operational excellence
- Efficiency – similar output cheaper than competitors
- Consistency – reliability, predictability, near-zero mistakes
- Exceptional levels of quality and continuous improvement

Harley-Davidson
BMW   Citibank
Disney   Apple   Coca-Cola   eBay

Modes of customer orientation
- Creating emotional associations with the customer
- Tailoring products/services to customer niches
- Consistently exceeding expectations

Ben & Jerry's   Dell   Amazon.com
Ikea   3M   Sony
Starbucks   First Direct

Modes of innovation
- Differentiation through continuous product/service innovation
- Creating a new organizational architecture that can be sustained as a differentiating factor

exemplified by SIA and Zara). A second aspect is consistency, reliability, predictability and near-zero mistakes (e.g., McDonald's, Toyota). A third aspect is the achievement of exceptional levels of quality and continuous improvement (e.g., Louis Vuitton, Bose).

Customer orientation has multiple aspects too. One aspect is the ability to create emotional associations with customers (e.g., Harley-Davidson, Coca-Cola). A second aspect is the ability to effectively tailor products and services to specific customer niches through a deep understanding of customers (e.g., Apple, Citibank, eBay). A third aspect is the ability to consistently exceed customer expectations (e.g., Disney, BMW).

Lastly, we consider innovation. There are companies that excel at consistently offering new products and services, either in an incremental fashion (e.g., Ben & Jerry's constantly offering new ice-cream flavours or Starbucks offering new coffee flavours and innovative delivery processes) or that are a combination of incremental and groundbreaking ones (e.g., Sony, 3M). A second aspect of innovation, which is more strategic in nature, is the ability to develop a new business model, a new organizational architecture (including systems, processes and values), that can be sustained in the longer term as a differentiating factor (e.g., Dell, Ikea, First Direct, Amazon.com).

It is not just the structural aspects of the business model that offer sustained success, since these can be copied by competitors, but rather the detailed internal systems, processes, interrelationships and cultural values that are developed over time. In Chapter 3, we depicted in an activity system map the internal fit and coherence of various organizational aspects that operationalize and enshrine SIA's core competency of cost-effective service excellence. Even if competitors were to copy any parts of this system, such as the holistic staff development or the strategic synergies aspect, they would only have a part of the puzzle, and they would also lack the specific cultural values that glue together these organizational arrangements.

If we consider the three classes of capabilities, we can say that SIA has developed all three to a higher level than most in its peer group, which would go some way towards explaining its outstanding performance over the years. With regard to operational excellence, we discussed in earlier chapters several factors that give SIA an edge over competitors in terms of efficiency and consistently superior quality. As regards customer orientation, we highlighted SIA's attention to delivering services that customers want and to gathering, analyzing, utilizing and responding to customer feedback to keep in touch with its market. As for innovation, we saw how SIA engages in continuous innovation as well as in maintaining a unique internal activity system that competitors find almost impossible to copy.

If we had to select one of the three classes of capabilities in which SIA really excels, it would be operational excellence, given the seamless execution of strategy in an efficient and consistent manner, the tight and coherent interconnections among the various organizational processes, and the consistently superior level of service.

Capabilities and core competencies are thus embedded in people, processes and culture. Companies have to be clear whether they have any capabilities that satisfy the four criteria (i.e., valuable to the customer, rare, hard to imitate and hard to substitute) and can therefore be regarded as their core competencies. If there is no clarity, then the links with strategy will also be unclear and strategic alignment will not be achieved. The advantage given by core competencies as differentiating factors can slowly be eroded if competitors invest in building similar competencies. Thus, a company has to continuously monitor competition and improve its own competencies to stay ahead.

Also worth noting is that investments in developing capabilities and competencies are often hard or impossible to evaluate using conventional criteria of return on investment and other financial measures. When SIA decided in 1972 to break from industry norms and compete on service excellence, the assumptions involved in computing costs and returns would make any numerical calculation at best incomplete and inaccurate, and at worst irrelevant. What was needed, rather, was a conviction, from the highest level, that this was the right thing to do, together with the ability to mobilize the organization in a coherent manner to actualize the vision. J. Y. Pillay, former chairman of SIA, gave an insight into SIA's decision to focus on superior service in an industry where service was lacklustre:

> Those were the days when most airlines in the region and around the world were heavily subsidized by their governments. SIA capitalized on that myopia. A subsidized entity is, almost by definition, a flaccid, supine organization. SIA, therefore, did not really have to face severe competition until the authorities in more and more countries got religion, the religion of the market economy. Then SIA had to work

more strenuously. A great advantage SIA enjoyed three decades ago was the ability to cock a snook at the competition. The major carriers in the industry, together with their camp-followers, suffered from a self-imposed constraint, through IATA, the International Air Transport Association, to offer uniform standards of service and fixed tariffs. Not being a member of IATA, SIA led the way in pioneering quality innovations in the cabin, allied to flexible pricing in the marketplace. That policy attracted the customers, boosted revenue and profit, and enabled SIA to modernize its fleet faster than the competition.... The competition eventually got wise to SIA's formula for success, and sought to emulate it. SIA's lead was attenuated, but by no means eliminated. That lead persists because of the high quality of internal dynamics within the organization. Organizational strategy plays no less important a role than corporate strategy.[8]

One important lesson is, therefore, the need to critically examine the company's capabilities, and carefully assess if they satisfy the four criteria, to find out whether the company has any capabilities that qualify as core competencies and that can provide competitive advantage. We often ask executives to think about such issues during our executive development work: What are their companies' core competencies, if any? Are these aligned with their market, strategy and operations? And will their companies be successful in future with these competencies? These are always interesting issues to consider, but never simple ones to answer.

Understanding Strategic Innovation

We discussed in Chapters 3 and 4 SIA's innovation processes, but they are not the whole story of SIA's success as a serial innovator. Extending the theme of innovation as a capability, we can now ask: What is it that makes innovation 'strategic'? We suggest that *strategic innovation* can be seen as an answer that differs from the usual response to the three basic questions of strategy: what, who and how. 'What' relates to both the product or service offered, as well as to positioning or unique selling proposition; 'Who' refers to the segments targeted; and 'how' refers to delivery channels as well as to the business model involved. Table 6–2 gives examples of strategic innovation in the airline and banking industries. In each case, budget airlines and virtual banking, respectively, at one time presented different, novel answers to these basic questions of strategy and created major headaches for the incumbents.

Is SIA a strategic innovator? If we begin by considering its early days, SIA did provide a different answer to the dominant industry approach in 1972, when Malaysia–Singapore Airlines split up into Malaysian Airline System and Singapore Airlines. The dominant industry approach involved offering low levels of service (constrained by stringent IATA rules) and emphasized issues such as safety and infrastructural robustness. According to Ian Batey, founder of Batey Ads, the company that developed and nurtured the Singapore Girl brand icon, at the time most Asian airlines "bowed under the pressure of the popular global commentary and consumer research in the early 1970s."

Table 6–2

Strategic innovation in the airline and banking industries

Strategic innovation dimension	Airline industry		Banking industry	
	Dominant answer	New answer	Dominant answer	New answer
What? (product and service)	Full-service air travel	Budget air travel	High street banking	Virtual banking
What? (positioning)	Differentiation, service level	Low cost, no frills	Differentiation (brand, reliability)	Differentiation (service level, convenience)
Who? (customers)	All segments	Primary target budget-conscious travellers	All segments	Primary target educated professionals
How? (delivery channels)	Air and ground infrastructure	Air and ground infrastructure	Branches, Internet, telephone	Internet, telephone
How? (internal architecture)	Flag carriers, focus on quality and innovation	Budget airlines, focus on leanness and efficiency	Full-service infrastructure	Call centres, Internet supported by full infrastructure

Both firmly called for a communications strategy that highlighted modern technical skills, modern aircraft, international experience, network size and Western pilots ... it was safe, conventional wisdom supported by substantial research data ... our team looked into the crystal ball and made a number of predictions. First, that all the national airlines of note would become increasingly homogeneous in terms of hardware benefits ... secondly, while reliability and modernity were important to customers, such attributes would eventually become basic 'givens' and the distinctive differential would increasingly relate to what goes on during the flight – the on-board travel experience, the personal service and the service-related comforts.[9]

This line of thinking both influenced, and was consistent with, the broad lines of thinking at SIA: sustainable competitive differentiation would come from superior service, a well-known and potent brand icon, and constant innovation. We shall discuss in the next section on 'fostering strategic innovation' several practices that further qualify SIA as a strategic innovator.

A related way to look at strategic innovation is to construct strategic groups maps of the industry and view the 'white spaces' as potential directions for innovation. In the strategic groups map shown in Figure 6–4 that presents selected competitors in the airline industry, the incumbents on the top right were surprised by the entry of budget airlines (bottom left) presenting a different answer to the basic questions of strategy – an answer that large segments of the market found very appealing. The responses of the incumbents have ranged from attempts to cut

Figure 6–4
Innovation as filling in the white spaces

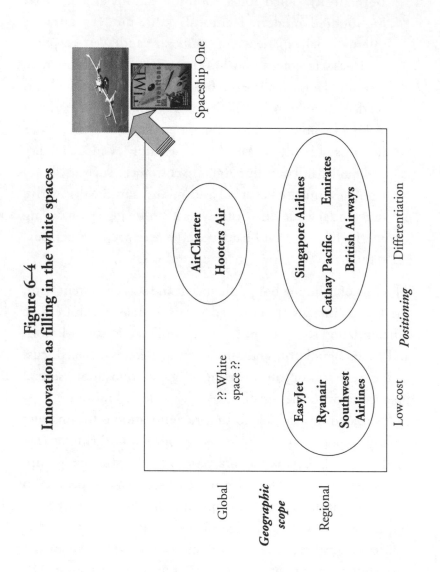

costs and setting up of subsidiary budget airlines (which have mostly failed because of conflict between the different business models); to attempts to strengthen differentiation and to conducting mergers with the hope that size would make up for inefficiency. In addition to budget airlines, smaller, niche companies exist on the bottom right of the map that offer services such as leasing or recreational flights.

This leaves a clear white space on the top left, which many believe would not be possible to fill. We believe, however, that it is only a matter of time before budget offerings for long-haul flights appear. In addition, and thinking out of the box (literally in terms of this figure), in a couple of years one may be travelling to the moon for around US$100,000 with the first commercial space flight company, which is supported by Paul Allen (co-founder of Microsoft) and Richard Branson (CEO of Virgin Group). The success of this venture in creating Spaceship One has created headaches for NASA (the US National Aeronautics and Space Administration), which needs substantially more resources to conduct space flights. In some five to seven years, prices for space flights are expected to fall to around US$15,000, expanding the potential market and making a trip to the moon an attractive option for celebrating special occasions or fulfilling one's dreams of space travel.

Earlier, we discussed two modes of innovation, relating to either the dimension of new products and services (the 'what') on the one hand or the dimension of a novel business model or organizational architecture (the 'how') on the other. New products and services can either be incremental expansion of existing offerings (e.g., new flavours of ice cream or new varieties of washing liquid) or they can offer significant added value as perceived by the customer (e.g., an MP3 player that is so successful that its name becomes synonymous with the product, an Internet search engine that seems to always find what users are looking for, an electronics company that periodically comes up with groundbreaking, market-driving products that create entirely new markets). If we combine these two dimensions, we can derive the following typology of strategic innovation shown in Figure 6–5.

Figure 6–5
A typology of strategic innovation

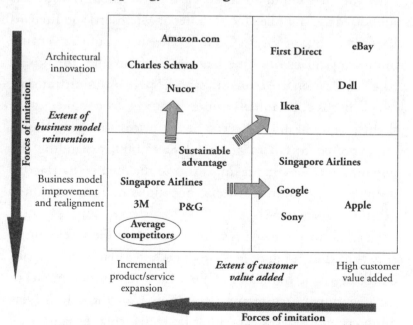

Leading companies that are strategic innovators need to keep in touch with the market and sustain innovative efforts in order to move towards the top right-hand side of the diagram (as the arrows in the centre of the figure indicate), as the forces of imitation continually pull companies towards the lower left point, where the average competitors are located. Leading companies also need to worry about strategic alignment and strive to create unique internal configurations (processes, systems, cultural values) that cannot be copied by competitors easily and that operationalize their core competencies, which in turn support their strategy. If all of this is in line with what the market wants, either explicitly or latently, then a winning combination is created.

Fostering Strategic Innovation

How can a company extend its chances of being a strategic innovator, and what are some practices that foster innovation? To begin with, there are several structured frameworks for managing innovation, one of which is shown in Figure 6–6.

Such frameworks are useful, but they apply mostly to what happens after the new ideas emerge and to intra-company processes rather than networks of innovation. A more vexing question is: How can organizations have higher chances of accessing and investing in novel, potentially valuable ideas before the bandwagon starts?

One way is engaging in 'ideas brokering', identifying and using existing ideas in new ways. Henry Ford was inspired by the assembly line used in meat packing and applied it to car

Figure 6–6
Managing innovation: Moving from an idea to cash

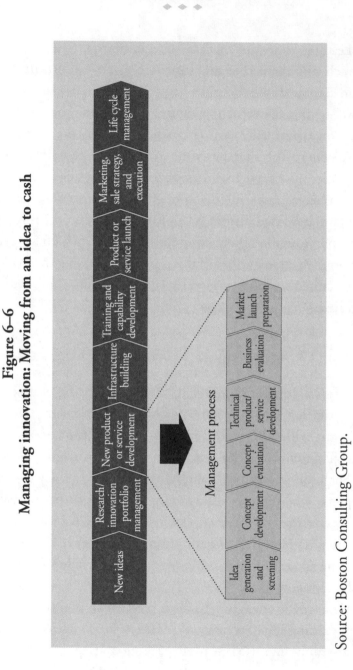

Source: Boston Consulting Group.

manufacturing, which was at the time an inefficient, craft-based production process that produced cars for the elite. The development of FAST (fully automated seamless travel) by SIA aptly illustrates idea brokering. Biometric technologies, which enable FAST, already existed in other domains; what SIA did was to identify and effectively apply these ideas to the aviation industry, as well as to integrate them with capabilities present in the company in related domains (e.g., SIA's system for real-time seat allocation and confirmation, the immigration automated clearance system in use at the Singapore–Malaysia border and the smart card used with the clearance system).

A related way of fostering innovation is to draw from inter-organizational networks and strategic alliances ideas and resources for developing a complex new offering. One example is Apple Computer's development of the iPod, which took only eight months from the start of the project to market entry. Apple only designed the user interface; everything else was supplied by a network of partners. The lion's share of the value, however, was captured by Apple, since it owns the iPod brand. SIA's development of FAST also illustrates the use of inter-organizational networks as a source of ideas and capabilities. FAST is at its core a collaborative effort of SIA, the Civil Aviation Authority of Singapore, the Immigration and Checkpoints Authority, the Singapore Police Force and the Ministry of Home Affairs that draws on the relevant technical knowledge of the government computer laboratories.

A third way to foster innovation is to develop or discover novel ideas through a deep understanding of the customer. The iPod was introduced after similar products were already available on the market (the first movers) – some of which had more extensive features and more advanced technology. However, it was Apple that got under the skin of teenagers with a sleek design, evocative advertising and promotions, and careful management of product availability, creating a 'cool' aura around the iPod that swiftly rendered it the market leader. SIA's new offerings (e.g., Krisflyer, Dolby sound, broadband Internet in the air) are the result of careful evaluation of customers' lifestyles, wants and needs coupled with extensive preparations and testing to ensure that their implementation is up to the usual high standards.

A fourth consideration is the need to create an internal culture and structure that supports innovation, learning and change. There has to be a clear call from leadership emphasizing the importance of innovation, role modelling by the most senior level of the organization, an evaluation and reward system that monitors and rewards innovation, dedicated roles for innovation-related activities such as idea brokering and network engagement, and dedicated spaces and events for idea exchange and cross-pollination. These have been pursued by SIA in different ways, as discussed in earlier chapters. The aim would ultimately be to create a learning organization, an organization with a flexible and adaptive culture and structure and an open mindset that encourages continuous change and development.

Executives therefore have to ask themselves: To what extent is my company a strategic innovator? Do we have a novel business model that cannot be copied easily? Do we continually offer novel products and services to the market that really add value? Do we engage in innovative behaviours and practices such as idea brokering and making use of inter-organizational networks?

Do we have the right culture, structure and processes in our company to foster innovation? If the answer to the above questions is not positive, alarm bells should sound.

The Role of the Institutional Environment

Can a company succeed simply because it is located at the right place? Some argue that SIA could not have been a market leader if it were located elsewhere. The institutional environment certainly plays a role in company success, and we will use Porter's diamond model of national competitive advantage to understand how being located in Singapore has been advantageous for SIA.

First of all, if a company can be successful in an environment where rivalry is intense, and if it follows robust strategies in that environment, then it has much higher chances of being successful elsewhere. SIA faces vigorous competition from regional rivals based in competing hubs (e.g., Cathay Pacific in Hong Kong, Malaysia Airlines in Kuala Lumpur, Thai Airways in Bangkok). Without the benefit of a national market, given the small size of Singapore, SIA was thrown into regional and global competition from day one – and without any direct state assistance. As J. Y. Pillay recounted, "One great advantage SIA enjoyed was that the authorities were scrupulous in observing a hands-off policy. They did what every far-sighted government should do, in the way of creating an efficient infrastructure, negotiating traffic rights, preserving labour peace, and so forth. But there was no interference with SIA, and no subsidies. SIA's guiding imperative was that nobody owed us a living. Call it confidence, pride, hubris, or whatever. We were determined to take on the competition entirely on our own."[10]

Secondly, if a company can satisfy very demanding and sophisticated customers, it means it has raised its service quality to a level which can stand up to the most able competitors in global markets. SIA has had to please very demanding customers, as service levels in Singapore are generally high and there are expectations of high quality when buying from the market leader. In addition, the relatively high economic growth in the region aided SIA in achieving higher returns, which were in turn invested in improving the level of service, such as renewing the fleet faster than competitors and developing a longer and more holistic cabin crew training programme than competitors.

Thirdly, the presence of related and supporting industries in Singapore with high levels of quality and sophistication has benefited SIA. Singapore being one of the most technologically advanced and wired nations in the world is a positive factor in SIA's adoption of technology, such as Internet-related and mobile phone services as well as the FAST project. The high quality of education in Singapore is another positive factor, which facilitates the implementation of high-standard development programmes for SIA employees. Lastly, perhaps it is no surprise that SIA was the first airline to introduce food on board that passengers actually enjoy, considering that Singapore is one of the acknowledged gourmet capitals of the world.

Fourthly, if a company can draw from ample and high-quality factors of production, it stands a better chance of becoming an effective competitor. Again, Singapore has offered a lot in this regard: availability of a motivated and educated workforce, a strategic location, high tourist demand, and an airport that is acknowledged as one of the best in the world. Figure 6–7 summarizes the environmental factors that have benefited SIA.

The Role of Culture

We have briefly noted some of SIA's cultural values in the preceding chapters. We will now highlight some salient ones that we believe underlie a lot of the practices that make SIA a winner in the intensely competitive aviation industry. Porter's diamond framework does not capture the role of culture (which is to be expected since Porter is an economist), but in this case it is worth addressing an issue that gradually became obvious to us: that several of SIA's key cultural values derive from the contextual, national culture.

To start with, in SIA there is a strong sense of collective destiny. This developed from SIA's early days, when employees knew that if the airline did not do well it would not be subsidized but would instead be closed down by its majority owner, the state. The feeling is sustained by the company's evaluation and reward policies that encourage peer pressure to perform. At the national level, the same sense of collective destiny has been cultivated over the years.

Secondly, there is a high level of organization and continuous drive for efficiency, values that characterize both SIA and Singapore. As discussed in earlier chapters, SIA emphasizes not only quality but also efficiency as well as seamless implementation. At the national level, the scarcity of resources

Figure 6–7
How the institutional environment benefits SIA

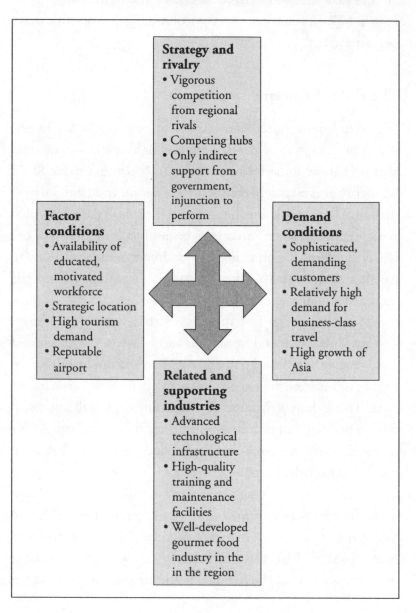

Strategy and rivalry
- Vigorous competition from regional rivals
- Competing hubs
- Only indirect support from government, injunction to perform

Factor conditions
- Availability of educated, motivated workforce
- Strategic location
- High tourism demand
- Reputable airport

Demand conditions
- Sophisticated, demanding customers
- Relatively high demand for business-class travel
- High growth of Asia

Related and supporting industries
- Advanced technological infrastructure
- High-quality training and maintenance facilities
- Well-developed gourmet food industry in the in the region

has meant that historically Singapore could only succeed by focusing on value-added products and services together with high levels of efficiency.

Thirdly, both SIA and Singapore believe in pragmatism. Decisions are taken on a 'what will work' basis, and decision makers readily acknowledge that something may not be working and a new solution may be needed. Both at SIA as well as in Singapore, there is a clear understanding that the world is changing and that current ways of thinking and the way things are done need to be continually reexamined.

A fourth common value is continuous improvement, in a substantive way – not just incremental improvements or rearrangements to give a superficial impression of improvement, but a real effort to continually look for ways to do things better. This is clear at both the national level as well as in SIA's internal policies and external offerings. Innovation occurs partly by inspiration, but mostly by an open search for ideas, a deep understanding of the customer, and sound internal development before a new-service introduction. SIA has been very effective at producing innovations that customers actually use and that can provide competitive differentiation, and the company is not sentimental about challenging and letting go of any outdated practices. According to Batey, "Once you become a global brand leader in both profits and reputation, there is a tendency to move to a defensive strategy, to protect your treasure, to look for safeguards, rather than retain the adventurous spirit that won you fame and fortune in the first place. In SIA's case, you can bet your bottom dollar that, while they have enjoyed amazing success, they will never waver in their tireless commitment to provide consumers with the best air travel experience in the world."[11]

The cultural value of continuous improvement at SIA can be better understood by considering the cultural background of Singapore. The historical evolution of the city-state is remarkable, transforming from a land of slums and poverty to a world-class metropolis in three decades. First, Singapore leveraged its location to become a trading and transshipment hub for cargo ships on their way to other parts of Asia. Then investment was pumped into manufacturing. Gradually, realizing that low value-added manufacturing would move to cheaper locations, the focus shifted to high value-added products and services – information technology, chemicals, biotechnology and finance. The current focus is on creating a learning nation and becoming a global schoolhouse, the place where anyone can go to receive quality education.

So, there is some truth to the suggestion that SIA is a market leader because it is based in Singapore. However, this would account for only a part of its success, and in no way devalues it, since national success is not achieved by chance either but is based on effective public policy decisions and investments. Some even believe that it is not the nation benefiting the airline but rather the other way round! "This is an unusual case of a national airline brand successfully helping to shape the global stature of its country, rather than the reverse!"[12]

What really matters at both the national and organizational levels are robust strategies, seamless implementation, and continuous vigilance and realignment when necessary. As J. Y. Pillay put it, "A credible and respected brand is the end-product of a long chain of strategies and initiatives, and disciplined execution, not the starting point ... SIA's goal from the outset was to offer superior service in every area, at a competitive price, while yielding a surplus to finance expansion and modernization, and to provide a satisfactory return to shareholders. All this while keeping employees satisfied, happy and motivated."[13]

In Conclusion

We have argued in this chapter that there is a need for firms to be clear about their generic strategy and that a combination of generic strategies is possible, that firms should strive to achieve high levels of strategic alignment and engage in realignment as needed, that they should nurture and invest in capabilities and core competencies that support their strategy, and lastly that they should understand what strategic innovation involves and strive to foster it. Our study of SIA has shown that, while these goals are incredibly difficult to achieve, they are the key ingredients of success. The organization that can play at this level can create near-unassailable advantages and extraordinary performance.

NOTES

[1] We will use concepts from Michael Porter, 'How competitive forces shape strategy', *Harvard Business Review*, March–April 1979, to summarize some of the salient features of the airline industry.
[2] Michael Porter, *Competitive Advantage: Creating and Sustaining Superior Performance*, New York: Free Press, 1985.

3 We use the term *low cost* here rather than *cost leader* since SIA is not a cost leader compared to low-cost carriers, although it is one when compared to its major competitors.

4 S. Kerr, 'On the folly of rewarding A while hoping for B', *Academy of Management Journal*, 18 (1975): 769–83.

5 For a detailed discussion of this situation, see L. Heracleous, 'The demise of foreign competitors in the Chinese beer industry', in K. Singh, N. Pangarkar and L. Heracleous, *Business Strategy in Asia*, Singapore: Thomson Learning, 2004.

6 For an idea of 'profit pool', see O. Gadiesh and J. L. Gilbert, 'Profit pools: A fresh look at strategy', *Harvard Business Review*, May–June 1998, pp. 139–47.

7 See B. Wernerfelt, 'A resource-based view of the firm', *Strategic Management Journal*, 5, no. 2 (1984):171–80.

8 Quoted from speech by Mr Pillay, chairman of the Singapore Exchange Ltd, at the Right Angle Seminar 'Rising Above the Crowd: Maintaining Your Presence in a Rough Marketplace', 15 March 2002.

9 Ian Batey, *Asian Branding: A Great Way to Fly*, Singapore: Prentice Hall, 2002, pp. 117–8.

10 See note 8.

11 Batey, p. 137.

12 Batey, p. 124.

13 See note 8.

Index

Note: The letters *f* and *t* followed by page numbers indicate figures and tables.

INDEX

◆ ◆ ◆